Charlotte Cole grew up in Cumbria and now lives in London. She is an editor at The Women's Press. She has edited *Sunrise to Sunset: An Anthology of Summer Reading* (1997), *First Frost: An Anthology of Winter Reading* (1998), and *Between You and Me: Real-life Diaries and Letters by Women Writers* (1998), all published by The Women's Press.

Helen Windrath is senior commissioning editor and rights manager at The Women's Press. She has edited *The Women's Press Book of New Myth and Magic* (1993), *Reader, I Murdered Him, Too* (1995), *Feast! Women Write About Food* (1996), and *Something to Savour: Food for Thought by Women Writers* (1996), all published by The Women's Press. She lives in London.

Also edited by Charlotte Cole and Helen Windrath from The Women's Press:

The Women's Press Book of New Myth and Magic (1993) ed Helen Windrath
Reader, I Murdered Him, Too (1995) ed Helen Windrath
Feast! Women Write About Food (1996) ed Helen Windrath (with Laurie Critchley)
Something to Savour: Food for Thought from Women Writers (1996) ed Helen Windrath (with Laurie Critchley)
Sunrise to Sunset: An Anthology of Summer Reading (1997) ed Charlotte Cole
First Frost: An Anthology of Winter Reading (1998) ed Charlotte Cole
Between You and Me: Real-life Diaries and Letters by Women Writers (Livewire Books for young women, 1998) ed Charlotte Cole

THE FEMALE ODYSSEY

Visions for the 21st Century

Charlotte Cole & Helen Windrath, editors

First published by The Women's Press Ltd, 1999
A member of the Namara Group
34 Great Sutton Street, London EC1V 0LQ

British Library Cataloguing-in-Publication Data
A catalogue record for this book is available from the British Library.

ISBN 0 7043 4613 3

Typeset in Scala 10/12pt by FSH Ltd, London
Printed and bound in Great Britain by Cox & Wyman Ltd,
Reading, Berkshire

CONTENTS

INTRODUCTION

The twentieth century has been one of tumultuous change, especially for women. And as women's lives have changed profoundly, the impact has been felt in personal relationships, the workplace and the wider political arena. But with tremendous leaps forward there is often a vicious backlash, and we then find ourselves repeating the same debates and fighting to defend gains we had assumed were securely ours. Yet our history is also one that shows the value of perseverance; how our tenacious desire for real, fundamental and lasting change is not easily diluted or assuaged. It tells the story of women's tremendous courage in the face of adversity across the centuries; an unbroken thread connecting us with generations of women who came before.

So, as the century draws to a close, we feel that this is an ideal time to assess where we have been and where we are going, to celebrate women's achievements, and share aspirations. We invited a number of leading women writers and activists to contribute to this book, and share their thoughts for the future, and we were in equal parts moved, delighted and inspired by the responses we received.

A number of the essays look at where we are now. Kate Mosse urges us to push the boundaries of our creativity constantly, not just at these supposedly significant points in time. Jenni Murray reflects on how, now women's roles have been transformed, it is the turn of men to change – and how this can start, practically, with boys' education. Kathy Lette, in her own unique way, talks about our self-obsessed quest for happiness. Rosalie Bertell argues the case for a new value system based on sustainability rather than the depletion of the Earth's resources. And June Jordan insists that it is up to us to work actively for change, if we want the future to be a better place.

However, some of the pieces aren't so positive. Judith Arcana's worrying women express concern about many things that will be familiar to all those with late twentieth-century angst, while Yasmin Alibhai-Brown takes a more personal look at the future, as she shares her hopes and fears for her children. Andrea Dworkin has some dreams for the next thousand years but, sadly, expects only nightmares. Nawal el Sa'adawi vigorously discusses the situation for women in the Middle East. And Bulbul Sharma looks at the gulf between the rich and poor in India, and wonders if it can ever be bridged.

Some of the writers have chosen to look to the past for inspiration: Emma Mashinini introduces her granddaughter Mphoentle, who draws strength from the way three generations of women in her family lived through Apartheid with dignity and helped change the face of South Africa. Anees Jung reflects on the life of her mother – a woman who has spent her life behind closed doors in the company of other women, and who is now looking with admiration at the very different lives of her daughters. And Caeia March tells of Women's Land – two acres influenced by women-only communities of the past, that are being tended and held in trust for the future.

Perhaps the most fun pieces are by those who have imagined glorious views of the future. Shelley Bovey envisages a world where fat has long been the norm, and we all eat healthily and with pleasure. Zelda Curtis pictures an era of shared living and responsibility. Vanessa Baird sends dispatches from the twenty-first century, where amidst the many constructive movements for change, much has already been achieved. And Mary Daly looks back at the twentieth century from a time and continent when patriarchy, and its accompanying destructive technology, have finally ceased to exist.

We hope you enjoy your journey through the hearts and minds of the writers we have gathered here. *The Female Odyssey* reflects the rich variety of women's experience, and our continuing quest – the odyssey of the title, perhaps – to make this planet a fairer and better place.

Charlotte Cole and Helen Windrath

CHANGING UP THE FUTURE OF WOMEN

June Jordan

This past Friday I underwent my third go-round with root canal surgery: third, that is, in ten days.

That's a lot, and I have to think about it. I don't suppose anyone plans to have root canal anything, any more than anyone plans to have a mastectomy. You can't schedule these catastrophes. But the shock of these emergencies, I think, could be handled better if you knew they hovered out there as possible attacks upon your sanity and poise, and if you therefore acted, as best you could, to prevent their crash arrival.

As far as I can tell, that would mean changing up your value system and the reasons why you do what you do. For women like me, that's a difficult message to decode.

For example, five years ago, I got curious about breast implants: I thought maybe they'd make me more desirable, or irresistible, or anyway, secure, in what was a consummately crazed and volatile love affair. And so I consulted a plastic surgeon who, after enumerating the obvious and not-so-obvious benefits of bigger and uplifted breasts, added one prerequisite: that I secure a mammogram, first, in order to confirm that my breasts were healthy.

This lone requirement led to the discovery of breast cancer and a consequent partial mastectomy that I have, this year, finally celebrated surviving.

Or, as my oncologist put it: 'Your vanity saved your life.'

So I am not about to pretend to disdain female

vanity in general, or mine, in particular.

But given the rapacious extent of the cancer that was identified and tracked all the way into my lymph nodes, maybe there could have been other, earlier, reasons why I decided to have a mammogram.

If I'd ever heard about the incredibly high incidence of breast cancer among women, and/or if I had known about the even more incredibly high mortality rates that obtain among women afflicted with breast cancer, then, maybe, I would have been seeking out regular mammograms over the past fifteen or twenty years, yes, and maybe, furthermore, I would have made it my business to join women nationwide to eradicate that killer! (I say 'maybe' because the inclinations of denial can be, sometimes, overwhelming.)

But I hadn't heard and I didn't know and so I simply thought I should try to look more appealing, you know, to somebody else, and, bam, there I was, totally surprised.

In the context of serious danger, totally surprised is not a good idea.

Two weeks ago, I found myself inside a watered-down rerun of that scenario. I went to the dentist to have my teeth cleaned because I am in this long-distance relationship and I am determined to ferret out advantages to long-distance romance. I mean, the disadvantages are pretty clear! What's good about it?!

Well, I'd decided that, as they say in all these 'other women' songs, one absolute advantage would be my never being seen unexpectedly. or in less than predetermined array, or with hair more than twenty-four hours beyond the ministrations of a beauty shop, and, for sure, I'd never ever be seen with dirty or stained teeth!

Having noted an upcoming reunion with my long-distance lover, a reunion pencilled on my calendar on a date not extremely far off, I therefore went to the dentist.

Once there, the hygienist flipped into emergency mode:

Apparently there was an ulcerated lesion on the roof of my mouth, for one thing, and for another, there might be quote non-vital unquote teeth contributing to that lesion, and so on.

Consequently, I have now submitted to two biopsies and three root canal surgeries and, would you believe, I still haven't seen that motivating long-distance lover?

But that's fine. Once again, in a sense, you might say, I've done the right things for, well, not wrong reasons exactly, but for reasons not altogether healthfully self-centered or politically conscious.

But how could political consciousness lead you to the dentist?

Well, an unhealthy mouth precludes a healthy loudmouth, and we need a whole lot more healthy female loudmouths out here. And that's not about to happen if we let a bunch of quote non-vital unquote situations take the teeth out of whatever we need and want to say.

This is not an argument against clean teeth. I'm fine with clean. But the difference between cleaning your teeth and root canal surgery is chasmic, and today I'm in favor of root canals.

But let me finish this true story.

So I had the first root canal surgery and much pain followed that.

In fact, the pain became just about unendurable and, therefore, last Tuesday I was on the phone throughout the night, calling for emergency medical help, and do you know what each dentist or physician told me at one a.m., and at three a.m., and at four a.m.?

Each of these health-care givers told me to take the pain-killer Vicodin. And so I took Vicodin and I took more Vicodin and I took more Vicodin, and the pain never subsided but I did verge into a serious over-dosed-on-Vicodin-incompetent-and-dizzy-and-helpless condition which, fortunately, a comrade asleep way the other side of Berkeley was willing to wake up and drive to my house to rescue me from.

As the syntax of that sentence should indicate, I'm saying Vicodin is not a great idea.

In the context of dangerous, disabling pain, drugs accomplish nothing except to further disable you. What's needed, instead, is an accurate diagnosis: What's the problem? Where is it located? And then you can extirpate the source of that pain.

I am not speaking against long-distance relationships, which, if they don't kill you with frustration, may, like vanity, sometimes save your life. But I am speaking against long distance from self-love and long distance from political love that would mean finding out what's quote non-vital unquote inside your mouth and anywhere else in your life, and then skipping past the purely cosmetic and/or the pain-killer routines so freely available to us and struggling, instead, for personal and political root canal extirpation of what's hurting us.

I believe that most women subsist with poisonous quote non-vital unquote factors packed into our mouths and our days and our nights; I am certain that most women wither and shrink and lower our voices and fold our hands and dissemble about how we feel. I know we endlessly prioritise how we look to somebody else because most of us subsist within a deadly long distance away from our pain and our desire, personal as well as political.

And because nobody likes a root canal.

*

So what's our problem? According to a 1980 United Nations' report on women, we constitute half of the world's population, but we put in two-thirds of the world's work hours, we receive one-tenth of the world's income, and we own less than one-hundredth of the world's property.

That's one description.

Here's another:

'At the age of 14 I just remember thinking I wasn't very good at anything, that I was hopeless. I couldn't understand why I was perhaps a nuisance to have around, which, in later years, I've perceived as being part of the [whole question of the] son. The child who died before me was a son and both [parents] were crazy to have a son and heir and there comes a third daughter. "What a bore, we're going to have to try again." I've recognised that now, and that's fine. I accept that.'[1]

Both of these descriptions beg the question, 'Why?!'

Why do we accept negligible income for our disproportionately hard, extended labor? Why do we accept less than negligible security of ownership in return for our invested energies which imbue ownership with value?

Or:

Why did Diana, Princess of Wales, accept that her parents regarded her birth as a failure/as a huge disappointment to their rightful expectation – of a son?

And:

What does it mean that our worldwide status quo remains abysmally poor, abysmally hostile to improvement, and abysmally powerless to extirpate universal sources for our suffering and debasement?

What does it mean to accept the hatred that makes

you hate yourself?

These are diagnostic questions.

How does it happen that the least valued human being everywhere is the very same woman who cleans the house that does not belong to her and who takes care of everybody who will never think to take care of her and who worries about pleasing those who despise her very presence and who tries
and tries and tries to make everything look 'nice'
and who tries and tries to satisfy the most wanton demands put upon her as to how she, herself, she, the least valued human being everywhere, should look inside the eyes of a mocking, cruel, exploitative, and basically indifferent, beholder?

Why is this normal?

Thirty-one years ago I wrote this poem, 'Okay Negroes':

Okay 'negroes'
American Negroes
looking for milk
crying out loud
in the nursery of freedomland:
the rides are rough.
Tell me where you got that image
of a male white mammy.
God is vague and he don't take no sides.
You think clean fingernails crossed legs a smile
shined shoes
a crucifix around your neck
good manners
no more noise
you think who's gonna give you something?

Come a little closer.
Where you from?

*

Thirty-one years later, I'm still asking: Where you from?

You/me/people of color/women and girls on the planet: Why do we accept a status quo that rejects our equal, our equally deserving, humanity? Are we waiting for a Fed-Ex delivery of our salvation? And who exactly is supposed to send that Top Priority Overnight Item to the door?

In a recent essay, 'Rwanda's Living Casualties',[2] the investigative journalist, Laura Flanders, re-examines the 1994 genocide that lasted three months, took the lives of a million people, and planned, and carried out, the rape of up to '500,000 women and girls in less than one hundred days'.

Flanders writes: 'Up to the present, in Rwanda as in Bosnia, most of those genocidaires stand a pretty good chance of getting away with murder. As for getting away with mass rape – their chances are better still.'

She describes her unwitting accommodation to the silence that permitted these crimes to unfold and the perpetrators to murder or bleed and torture and violently expel or horribly jolt raped women into a 'living death' because no one else – not the organised American women's national community, nor the African American national community, nor the Clinton Administration, nor the international media – did anything but fade on this enormous horror, and then click off our international TV screen consciousness.

And in one of the most unforgettable passages of this piercing report, Flanders tells us that Rwandan women who have survived that genocidal campaign of mass rape, have this to say:

'They wanted us to die of sadness.'

As for sadness and the future of women, let me share with you parts of this prose poem by the amazing poet, Sara Miles:

Thinking about sadness

There are places in the desert still named Badwater: someone left her bones here, someone drank from the alkaline spring. I was thinking of sadness and water under the bridge. I was thinking of temper and grief and then there was that badwater, that sadness, running darkly down the hill: you could stop there to drink and die of it

You could die dipping your fingers into that bad water . . .

I was thinking about walking ten paces behind the world holding the hand of sadness. I was thinking about the averted gaze. I was thinking about voices too sad to be heard. I was thinking there was bad blood bad water sad water between us and we were drinking it shrinking into it and rolling darkly away from the hill.

You could lose a temper to sadness. You could carry necessities across the desert and just lay them down. By the water. Lose a vision lose focus forget to lose temper in that shallow quicksand river, that sad thing, that restraining down-dragging wet sad quiet thing. You could lose real grief and not notice you were drowning . . .

I was watching wasted water run darkly down another's face. I was thinking of tears in the sand and the fierce companionship of thirst. There are places in the desert named Deliverance; Good Hope: I was walking with my eyes up holding the hand of an angry woman. I was thinking of sadness, its bones bleached behind us; I was walking with a speaking woman, we were walking past silence; I was thinking about sadness, evaporation, the trail.

In another recent essay, this one entitled 'Welfare and Work', by the peerless Frances Fox Piven,[3] we learn about the real deal economics behind punishing the poor – who are disproportionately female and disproportionately women and children of color.

Piven shreds the perversely popular rhetoric about both welfare and work in the United States. Behind the pieties, the catchphrase castigations of these poorest of poor American women, Piven finds and illuminates the economic interests served by such shameless cruelty and abuse. She writes: '...women barred from welfare aid will compete in a segment of the labor market which is already saturated with job seekers, with the result that wages for those who are already earning little will be driven down.'[4]

Overall, Piven argues, '...a politically mobilised business community is raising profits by squeezing wages, and using its formidable influence to change public policies so as to bolster its efforts. From this point of view, welfare cutbacks are associated with seismic shifts in the power relations between employers and employees. Of course, they are only a component of a much larger class strategy, a business war against labor.'

I ask you to backtrack a moment and notice how 'seismic' and 'large' and 'class shifts' and other acts of war begin and end on the backs of women who, meanwhile, possess the meanest set of alternatives to choose between: life-destroying penury on 'welfare' or life-destroying penury on lower and lower wages for more and more humiliating, and futile, punishing quote work unquote.

If, as Piven warns, these forced workers are not then legally recognised as workers and, therefore, not protected by Federal law, then anti-welfare vigilantes will have created an ancillary social disgrace. As Piven explains, '...in the absence of these protections, workfare means the creation of a virtually indentured labor force of welfare recipients'.

And so I ask again: How come?

When Clinton's Welfare 'Reform' rose into public view, where was the mobilised national women's community and where was the mobilised African American community, and the national community of Latinos, and elderly Americans, and children's rights' activists, and how come The Personal Responsibility Act has now been implemented, which will no longer allow education and job training to count as 'work' and will, therefore, undeniably, lock poor people into poverty – especially women and especially the nine million children dependent upon hopelessly impoverished American women?

How come?

There is a god-awful crisis on the way: actual poor women will soon become recklessly less able to resist the burdens of impoverishment, less able to overcome challenges of illness, irrelevant education, a dearth of childcare options, unemployment, and the calculated evaporation of public housing to shelter them. This crisis for poor women in our country will erupt and worsen and accelerate into worsening consequences for them, and for the rest of us, and it has already begun.

And, meanwhile, there was something called A Million Black Women's March, quite recently, and anywhere from 300,000 to one and a half million Black women converged in Philadelphia.

They said, 'We are standing, we are unified' but, as far as I can tell, there was not a single solitary piece of paper circulating for signatures to demand a single solitary anything, for example, A Government Responsibility Act to thwart the cruelty and the shamelessness of the ongoing, and intensifying, war against the poor:

Not one.

Three hundred thousand plus women standing, unified, in one place, and no political purpose to that gathering, no specific outcry for rescue funds for public education and rescue for job training and retraining, and no specific petitions to drastically stiffen state and Federal penalties for violence against women, even though poor Black women are, by far, those women most victimised by violence in our homes and on our streets: not one petition?!

So what was the idea, really?

To look bigger than ordinary and to gain an uplift of spirit that looks 'good' in photographs of that one-day event?

I think that was a waste of a fabulous opportunity for women's power: a de facto grass roots' defusion of justified fury.

Black women traveled long distances hoping to find themselves intersected with other Black women hinged to some finally spoken out loud purpose that would, at once, transform both the personal and the political future of their lives.

But there was no utterance of such a purpose.

And the future doesn't bode well for a second summoning of Black women who will have to puzzle through the apolitical weirdness of the first.

And in the same papers full of the news of Black women standing together under the rather odd motto of 'Repentance, Resurrection, Restoration' – I mean 'odd' given the verifiable victimised history of Black women to date – there was the story of 16-year-old Lo Eshe Lacy, a popular Black teenager killed by a drive-by bullet as she sat in the back of a parked van, hanging out with friends.

Six hundred people attended the funeral service for Lo Eshe, and one of them remarked that she thought it would help 'if we could let them know we love them while they are alive'. By 'them' she meant Black kids, and Black girls, especially.

I couldn't agree more. And I don't see how the Million Black Women's March let Lo Eshe Lacy know anything usefully specific about Black love for Black girls because nobody at the March spoke on Black violence in Black communities – whether that violence is so-called 'domestic' or whether it's omnipresent and a matter of a lousy crapshoot with your apparently incidental life at stake.

So far I've been laying down examples of show or no show:

No show for the neediest women and girls among us and, on the other hand, show for the sake of show, show for the sake of trying to seem unitedly harmless and more desirable: smiling clean teeth in a mouth that aches for root canal or/and trying to look big and uplift your image when, in fact, there's an economic and a political and a cultural cancer that requires extirpating surgery if something good, something healthy, is to emerge, survive and prosper.

It's really hard to accept the consequences of hatred and, also, that there is that hatred, simultaneously. So, mostly, we don't. Mostly, I think, we accept or accommodate to the consequences and we deny the hatred behind them. It's pretty difficult to come into the world female, and just a baby in fact, and suddenly there you are: a vulnerable creature weighing less than ten pounds and completely dependent upon grown men and grown women who will almost never run around shouting, 'It's a girl! It's a girl!'

It's difficult, and I think that our understandable wish to deny the ubiquitous, institutionalised, hatred arrayed against us because we are female human beings or because we are Black human beings, our understandable wish to deny the outside hatred that deforms and interdicts the otherwise freely beautiful and infinite future trajectories of our now hate-bedevilled lives, is a wish we will have to relinquish, resolutely, and then smother with our own frail breath. Or we will perish under the assault of predictable, punishing jeopardies we cannot, reasonably, hope to escape.

I know this is true. I know this is very hard.

And I believe this exceedingly difficult revision of our traditional female survival strategies has become clear, strangely enough, in the life and death of Diana.

The woman for whom sixty million flowers were chosen and carried and laid to rest in tribute to her own outreach to the world beyond her unearned privilege, that woman had, not so long ago, described herself as stricken by 'a feeling of being no good at everything and useless and hopeless and failed in every direction'.[5] And even as she articulated that tangle of tormented emotions for her own deliverance, I believe that she spoke for women and girls who confront and somehow co-exist with, or else simply seek to pacify, those horrible feelings inherent to female identity.

I know that she spoke for me: 'no good' 'useless' 'hopeless' 'failed'. From the moment of the news of the car crash in Paris I entered into continuing, close phone contact with two of my best friends who live in London. They are both first generation immigrants to England: Shaheen Haq from Pakistan and Pratibha Parmar from India, by way of Uganda.

Shaheen is Muslim and Pratibha is Hindi.

They are Black Londoners. And, as the first days after the crash progressed, I listened to their words weighed with such a tenderness and such a welling up of sorrow and loss that I became amazed. And so were they: amazed by the passion of their felt connection to Diana and crying, openly, over the phone, and plotting where to stand to make their witness to the passing of Diana.

And this is an excerpt from the letter that I sent to them, 7 September 1997:

Dearest Pratibha and Shaheen:

I watched the British coverage of the funeral procession and service for Diana, British time. So I am a bit punchy this morning, but I am glad of that minimal joining with you at this moment of grief yet to be understood, and honored.

It seems to me that the folks captured by the TV became 'whiter' and whiter, and that the folks in attendance at Westminster were, with the exception of three persons, all white, and I thought, well, that is what she was up against, really: monumental hypocrisy and monumental disregard of anyone outside the neanderthal mold of 'royal' and of 'English' self-imagery. We see what that colossal complacency, that depthless refusal to acknowledge anyone real, and complicated, and complicating the true picture of our common situation, here, in the world, we see what that did to 'England's rose' and so, we tremble for ourselves: if she who possessed such privilege could not catapult her vision and her desires into a safe place for happiness, how then shall we carry hope for our own happiness, our own safety, in our hearts?

What is ultimately remarkable, I believe, is that we do carry that hope, and that, in fact, we, the forcibly invisible and set aside, have always been the origin as well as the objective of that saving spirit...We embody the grief as well as the wish

> for love that could, day after day, break boundaries and rules that, as we know to the bone of our being, will, otherwise, kill us.
>
> And I write to salute you for the everlasting sweet trust of your presence on the planet. You are anything but invisible to me . . .

Writing from my heart I made, I think, a serious mistake. I said nothing about power.

And, alas, that is not surprising.

We, women, we know about coming together in grief.

We know about coming together against loneliness.

We know about coming together in love, and in acts of committed, reliable kindness.

But we, women, we still do not know about and crave and insist upon coming together in power for power.

Coming together for a specific, collective, political purpose, each and every time we convene a meeting of as many of us as we can persuade to stand or sit together, united.

Power for the power to recreate the world as a universal safe house for our highest aspirations and our universally neglected, or forsaken, human rights.

But, of course, there are exceptions to our general timidity, our usual deference, or surrender, to traditions that shadow the best implications of our female persistence.

Certainly there are women who pursue and who exercise and who develop power in ways inspiring beyond dispute.

The Burmese Nobel Peace Prize Laureate, Aung San Suu Kyi, is one such inspiration.

India's so-called 'Bandit Queen', Phoolan Devi, is another.

The record-setting victory of Mary McAleese, new

president of Ireland, elected with 59 per cent of the vote, is another.

And, closer by, if we're looking for a straight-up, unbelievably invincible woman all about her power to live?

This, from the *San Francisco Examiner*, 7 October 1997:

> Teen prostitute survives brutal hammer attack
>
> A teenage San Francisco prostitute is recovering from a fractured skull after being beaten, bound, stuffed in a car trunk, then thrown into the Bay, police say.
>
> The 19-year-old woman, whose name was not released, was in a stable condition at San Francisco General Hospital Tuesday after undergoing surgery.
>
> Police said she probably survived because she faked death during the ordeal.
>
> According to police reports, the incident started Saturday night when a man picked up the prostitute at 19th and Capp Streets and she agreed to have sex with him.
>
> The man drove to a parking lot in the Bayview District and demanded that she perform sex acts and that she kiss him. When she told him she didn't want to kiss him, the man became upset, grabbed her by her hair and slapped her, police reports said.
>
> He tied her by the wrists and forced her to perform fellatio. Police said she was forced nude to the rear of the car, where the assailant took a hammer from the trunk and hit her over the head several times.
>
> '[She] said she was so scared and thought she was going to die,' a police report said. 'She then said that she faked that she stopped breathing and fell to the ground.'

> The man put a plastic bag over her head, placed her into the trunk and drove to a car wash, where he washed his car...
>
> He drove her to the north side of Pier 9 and threw her into the water, police said. She was able to remove the plastic bag and swim to shore and, naked and bleeding from wounds to her head, got to the Embarcadero, where a passing motorist picked her up.

I feel incredibly inspired and revved, by that anonymous teenage heroine's resistance to hatred and the mutilating violence that follows from that hatred.

I feel incredibly inspired by 27-year-old Malika Saada Saar, who graduated from Brown University, cum laude, and then graduated from Stanford University's teaching program of studies and service and then jumped into the streets around her and then founded and now directs the San Francisco Family Rights and Dignity organisation because she simply couldn't believe and she simply would not accept that there was, in fact, no agency dedicated to the assistance and empowerment of homeless women with children – until she came along and invented one.

I feel incredibly inspired by Korean American, Mary Chung, not yet 30 years old, who is the founder and the president of the first, ever, National Asian Women's Health Organisation which now boasts an annual operating budget of 1.2 million dollars.

I feel incredibly inspired, and revved, by my colleague Julianne Malveaux's 7 September 1997 column headed 'Working Women Look to Unions for Help'. Malveaux presents this startling, major information: '...the American Federation of Labour – Congress of Industrial Organisations (AFL-CIO) exists as "the nation's largest working women's organisation" because it represents 5.6 million working women.'

And in the very heartland of America:

The 2 million dollar new housing complex for Native peoples with AIDS – a Minneapolis miracle of architecture, social conscience, cultural integrity, and health emergency management entirely thanks to the dauntless leadership of Sharon Day, an Ojibwe Native American who means what she dreams about.

The 1997 25th Anniversary of the University of Minnesota Women's Studies' Department that, chaired by the exceedingly able and modest Professor Jacquelyn Zita, has inaugurated a doctoral program, from September 1998.

The 1997 re-election of Sharon Sayles Belton, the first African American Mayor of Minneapolis.

The relentlessly feminist, and fully progressive, media investigations of Laura Flanders.

The indefatigable scholarship and theoretical envisionings of Frances Fox Piven.

The thrilling willingness of 300,000 plus Black women to gather together in one place at one time because maybe maybe maybe something worthy of their shoulder-to-shoulder faith might come of it.

– All, all, all of these living facts of ambition, dedication, and on-your-feet possibilities for revolutionary commitment seem to me extremely encouraging of huge hope, huge activist solidarity, huge coalitional exploration!

But perhaps the most exemplary, the most courageous news about the future of women appears in a *Newsday* article:[6]

> A 7-year-old Jamaican girl fought back tears as she testified in Queens Criminal Court yesterday against the man she says sexually assaulted her.
>
> Milton Jones, 37, who is representing himself in

> the trial, watched from across the courtroom as the girl testified that he assaulted her while living with her mother.
>
> The girl testified that Jones, who had lived with the family for three years, sexually assaulted her on two separate occasions between March and July, 1996.
>
> She smiled and appeared at ease as she took the stand, but minutes into her testimony, the girl, whose identity is being withheld because of her age, broke down in tears.
>
> After a short recess that allowed the girl to talk with someone the prosecutor described as a 'support person', she again took the stand and, wiping away tears, described what happened...
>
> Wearing a yellow quilted vest and a shirt that was untucked from his pants, Jones cross-examined the girl, who appeared composed as she again recounted what happened.
>
> 'Why would you sit here in front of God and everybody and say that my body parts touched yours?' he asked her.
>
> ''Cause I know the truth,' she replied.

She wiped away her tears.
She was no longer smiling.
She knew the truth.
She told the truth because she could not and she would not
separate the consequences of hatred from that hatred, itself.
She denied nothing vital to her healthy life.
At last there was no distance between
the truth that she must face
the truth that she must tell
and the truth of the lying, hideous
source for her tears.

There was no long distance left.
There was only that stunning, intimate,
and, also, public and, therefore, political
confrontation between the truth of her self
and the truth of the hatred that would
otherwise
destroy her human being.
And so she spoke up.
And she is seven years old.
And I, for one, would follow her lead.
No more Vicodin!
No more asinine anodynes!
No standing!
No to this ridiculous, shameful status quo!

Let's go!

Notes

1 *People*, 13 October 1997.
2 Laura Flanders, 'Rwanda's Living Casualties' in *Ms* magazine, March/April 1998.
3 Frances Fox Piven, 'Welfare and Work' in *Social Justice*, Spring 1998.
4 Citing another paper, 'Cutting Wages by Cutting Welfare', written by Lawrence Mishel and John Schmitt, Piven indicates that 'wages for the bottom 30% of workers will fall by 11.9 per cent. In California the drop will be 17.8 per cent and in New York, 17.1 per cent.'
5 *New York Times*, 1 September 1997.
6 Robert Ratish, 'Girl, Speaks of Sex Abuse' in *Newsday*, 7 October 1997.

PRE-MILLENNIUM TENSION

Kathy Lette

The human race is suffering from chronic PMT – Pre-Millennium Tension. And symptoms will persist until the turn of the century.

It's as though the world is turning into a Giant Missing Persons bureau. Everyone is trying to '*Find Themselves*'. If a sobbing celebrity on Oprah Winfrey announces that he or she is headed for 'new frontiers', you can be sure the journey will be 'inward bound'. Yep, the *Star Trek* series of the future will have our heroes battling negative karma and braving the uncharted depths of the psyche.

From American chat shows on one side of the Atlantic, to Fergie's confessional interviews on the other – the talk is of Happiness. The lack of, the yearning for, the right to ...

The 'Pursuit of Happiness', enshrined in the Declaration of American Independence, has become a Western addiction. A plethora of garrulous gurus, pseudo swamis, colonic irrigationists and karma maintenance mechanics now dominate our lives. The majority of us seem to belong to minority groups. Tom Cruise and Nicole Kidman's 'Scientology'; Fergie's Madame Vasso and her 'pyramid-healing'; Hilary Clinton's 'channelling workshops'; Richard Gere and Boy George's Designer Buddhism; and almost the entire male population of northern America flocking to 'Iron John' seminars to hug trees and 'get in touch with their fundamental masculinity'. (Personally I've never known a man who can keep his hands *off* his 'fundamental masculinity'...)

I think it's the idea of '*pursuing*' happiness I find so repugnant. I can understand people pursuing a promotion, an outlaw, that lying bastard who didn't tell you he was married until you found the teething ring in his pocket and who still owes you fifty quid...hey, like, how can I help? But the trouble with the pursuit of *happiness*, is that it's a little like the pursuit of the female orgasm. You get so concerned about whether you're having one or not, that you can't tell whether you are or not. Then, when you think you may be *having* one, there's only one thing on your mind – *is it as good as what everyone else has?*

Happiness is more at home in some cultures than in others. For Americans, with their world-renowned irony deficiency, 'feel good factors' and sound-bite politics, 'happiness' is mandatory. This is a country where people say 'have a nice day'...and then shoot you. If Jim Carrey is anything to go by, Canadians seem quite happy – then again, it could be a chemical imbalance. Australians tend to be accidentally happy. It's a combination of our – not work, but *shirk* ethic (we're phenomenally lazy) chronic septicaemia and good weather. (In that climate, it's impossible *not* to Give Good Hedonism.)

The British, on the other hand, seem far too masochistic to ever be 'happy'. If Britain had a constitution, 'the pursuit of *misery*' would be enshrined. I'd just like to remind you that this is the only country in the world which had a revolution, then *asked the Monarchy back*. And you don't get more masochistic than that! Even the euphoria of a Labour victory wasn't enough to change the mandatory dress code for the British – not rose, but morose-coloured glasses.

But the cult of happiness is extremely contagious

and even catching on here. In the PR battle between the Prince and Princess of Wales, the Princess was deemed to have won because she was seen as being the Most Miserable. After her famous Panorama interview, British public sympathy for 'the Queen of people's hearts' polled at 85 per cent – which must have had the Royal Family laughing; the sort of laughter which usually goes with a padded cell and a straitjacket.

'The pursuit of happiness' is used as a justification for the most appallingly selfish behaviour. Think of all the MMMs (Middle-aged Married Men) who trade in wives who've passed their amuse-by dates, for younger models. Membership of the 'First Wives Club' is full to overflowing, thanks to the 'unhappiness' of Bruce Springsteen, David Mellor, Donald Trump, Sylvester Stallone, Phil Collins, Clint Eastwood and all the other millions of men who think monogamy is something you make dining room tables out of.

As we approach the end of the century, unhappiness has become the psychological leprosy of the day. Something to be *cured*. But for sceptics like me, people who think that optimism is an eye disease, what's needed is a cure for all this self-indulgence – a Betty Ford Clinic for those addicted to the 'pursuit of happiness'. A twelve-step programme to wean the gullible off their gurus and men off their matrimonial kleptomania.

It's not that I have anything against happiness. It's just that self-liberation often becomes a substitute for commitment to political causes and social change. MI5 and the CIA, in fact, may soon be obsolete. Everyone I know is now a personal and very private eye. Besides, the truth about all this *fin de siècle* self-obsession, is that by the time you find yourself... *there's nobody home.*

MEN'S LIB FOR THE MILLENNIUM?

Jenni Murray

The twentieth century will, without doubt, be viewed by historians as the Women's Century. A girl born in 1899, as my grandmother was, had little chance of evading the role that was considered her destiny – to marry young, stay home and raise a family. Her forbears in the late nineteenth century had struggled hard to improve her chances of an education. Campaigners like Millicent Fawcett and Elizabeth Garrett Anderson had carried out a personal and largely peaceful struggle to open professions like medicine to women. Yet still only the privileged few, whose fathers or husbands were enlightened enough to permit it, got a foot on the ladder of opportunity. The suffragists argued powerfully, but peacefully for the vote. To no avail.

The floodgates opened on women's anger at their oppression during and after the First World War. Out went peaceful protest and in came the suffragettes. We won the vote and a voice in the decision-making process. From that point women, no matter how hard the establishment tried, could not be silenced. There were those like my gran – and subsequently my mother – who were in no position to take advantage of the changing climate. In a small mining village in Yorkshire the politicisation of the female population created barely a ripple until the vagaries of the miners' strike in the eighties drove them into collective action and later the need to become breadwinners. Yet the women in my family were part of a line of tough Yorkshire matriarchs who ran the home and the family budget with the cool efficiency and high moral standards of a Mother Superior. And in the Second World War they did their bit, taking in evacuees and working in the food office while women in other parts of the country took on the tasks that only men were believed capable of carrying out. Heavy factory work, driving huge vehicles, arduous agricultural duties – there was nothing by the end of the war that women couldn't do to keep a country running smoothly.

There were a few glitches in the fifties and sixties when the national mood demanded a return to the domestic status quo. The returning soldiers were to be given jobs and women again would keep the home fires burning. A significant number, though, liked their brief taste of freedom. One old friend told me her first wage as a war worker acted on her like a drug, she couldn't give it up. And in the family some of these wives and mothers wanted to renegotiate the old order. They argued for a form of democracy in the home where rights and responsibilities would be equally shared. In the workplace they wanted equal rights, equal opportunity and equal pay. The lives of my mother and grandmother remained unchanged – they continued to be devoted to their domestic responsibilities, but when my turn came they pushed and cajoled me through an education system and into a job market to which they believed I had every right. It never occurred to me, with their encouragement, that I was anything other than an equal citizen. At every turn my generation reaped the benefit of the activism of the previous one. As I joined the work-force in the seventies there came legislation on equal pay and sex discrimination. We could go to work in trousers, choose sex before marriage without fear of unwanted pregnancy and keep our jobs if we went on to have babies.

What has characterised the modern women's movement has been its ability to put everything up for discussion. And the crucial question that has been most hotly debated has been what it means to be a woman. We've examined what we wear. Shall it be dungarees, trousers, long skirts, short skirts, lipstick, high heels, flatties? We've concluded anything goes. Should we shave our legs and armpits, be thin or fat? Conclusion: whatever you want. Do we go out to work or stay at home and raise children? Whichever you choose. Can girls study maths and physics? Of course they can. Why are they doing badly? Not enough attention to the way they learn – provide it. They do better. In every arena, in every sphere, women have attended to their kind and made a difference.

Why have boys and men not done the same? As I look through the papers this morning, there are articles claiming to prove men don't iron because they're genetically programmed to be bad at such practical tasks. (Funny how they seem to be good at putting on plugs and lavishing tender loving care on their cars, but can't straighten out a shirt.) There are pictures of footballers who've come home drunk and given their nearest and dearest a beating, stories of racist hooligans throwing bottles at each other, even a former minister in the government who's slapped a female colleague at work – and I wonder again why, when we've liberated ourselves from the stereotypes that made us victims and domestic servants, are men still so bound by their old, outdated image? Me Tarzan – you Jane.

I suppose when you've been the powerful elite for such a long time there's little to drive you to examine your own gender. On the few occasions when it has occurred, in books by David Thomas and Neil

Lyndon, the tone has been bitter and mealy mouthed. Not a 'Hey the world is changing – where are the benefits for us chaps?', but a misogynist's view of modern mores – 'Why is this monstrous regiment doing us out of our jobs and refusing to wash our socks?'

But can men really be content with such a prescribed role in life? 'Flog yourself through education, get a job or a profession, my lad, hitch yourself to a millstone for the rest of your life and live to loathe and resent her and her offspring for the drain on resources they'll become. And should she dare to become a bit uppity, slap her down or change her for a fresher model.' What kind of basis for a relationship is that?

The sense that boys are different begins at the beginning, in the delivery room. Friends who've had daughters confirm the suspicion that the response from doctors and midwives, indeed anyone who happens to be around at the birth, is 'Oh, how sweet, look, you've got a lovely little girl.' I know from personal experience that birth of a son sounds like a much more significant event. 'Oh – what a great big handsome boy.' It's there in the words themselves and in the tone of voice – and the baby may not understand the language, but the quality of the sound must make an impact. As they grow, and a number of research papers have demonstrated this, the boys are encouraged to make noise, push buttons, climb trees, occupy a big space. How often have you heard 'Oh, boys will be boys'? And when's the last time you heard a girl encouraged to push herself to her physical limit?

Restrictive practices have been bad for girls, giving them no acceptable chance to explore their own courage and physical capabilities without being dubbed a tomboy. Equally, it's been bad for boys to assume that they'll enjoy kicking a football or sort out their differences with their fists. Where have been their opportunities, for instance, to play around with dress? Girls can now wear pretty party frocks or jeans and no one bats an eyelid, but a boy in a skirt – forget it. David Beckham, one of the footballers in the 1998 World Cup Team, went out with his girlfriend one night wearing a sarong. The response of the press? He was derided as a big girl's blouse.

I remember very clearly when my older son was around five going to buy him a new pair of shoes. Clarks at the time were heavily advertising a range of girls' footwear called Little Princess Shoes. If I remember correctly the gothic TV ad, a girl put on the shoes and, wearing them, overcame a number of obstacles to find the key to a hidden treasure chest. The shoes had a little fake diamond on the front and a tiny heel. In the shoe shop my little boy turned up his nose at all the sensible trainers on offer, and said no, he wanted the Princess Shoes. 'But you can't have those,' said the salesman, horrified, 'those are for girls.' With a sense of righteous indignation the diminutive hero turned around. 'If I was a girl,' he said, 'you wouldn't tell me I couldn't wear trainers. I can't see the difference.' The man became almost apoplectic when I bought him the shoes. They didn't last long – they were abandoned when he realised how uncomfortable they were for running across the park – so it cost me another pair of shoes. But I'm glad I stuck with him, let him try out his fantasy and express, maybe, just for that short time, his 'feminine' side.

Schooling was a problem. I can't tell you how many secondary schools we visited and asked the same question. This was 1993, and all we wanted to know was how were the schools tackling gender. It didn't matter whether they were all boys or mixed, state or private – the usual response was a blank look. A couple said they were trying to get more 'ladies' on the staff, but only one had even an inkling of the kind of problems this generation of boys would face in the future if they were not helped to think differently about themselves. How would they cope with a workplace where men and women were equal in number? How would they juggle their work and home life? How would they negotiate relationships with young women who were very different in outlook from their mothers and grandmothers? The school we finally chose told us that in the first form they'd be discussing housework – who does it and who should do it. By the sixth form they'd be preparing boys for university – thinking about cooking, laundry, addressing the issue of date rape. It was a start.

My partner has done his best to weather the storms of being an active father. He was a naval officer when we had our first child, and was made much fun of when he became the first – and I suspect the only – man to change his son's nappy on a submarine during a families' visit. When we couldn't stand any more childcarers living in the house, he quit his job and became a full-time dad, facing suspicion in the playground and finding it difficult to make the kind of support networks women form as a matter of course. It was a lonely time for him – then slowly a few more men joined him, either by choice or redundancy, as a generation realised their sex didn't necessarily guarantee them a job for life. At parties and social gatherings, though, I often heard him making up a home-based business for himself. He'd learned very quickly that people would turn away with boredom if he presented himself as just a 'father'.

So what's my dream, my utopia for the millennium? That men begin to ask the kind of question that to women has become second nature, as we all strive to understand the meaning of gender. And to ask it for themselves in school, universities, clubs and places of work, not relying on a handful of high-profile media women to do it for them. And to ask it for the positive reason that they too want to change, not because they're forced into it by 'uppity women' who've got out of hand.

There are it seems to me as many forms of masculinity as we have found there are of femininity. Men can be tough or gentle, ambitious or timid. They might be a demon on the rugby field or prefer to curl up at home with a good book. Some drive fast and hard, others cautiously and slow, some think about sex every second, others hardly think about it at all...just like women. I want men to be free to make the same kind of choices women are now able to enjoy and to make themselves suitable partners and colleagues for our daughters. Let's not see another generation of partnerships at home or at work stretched to breaking point on the rack of unmatched expectations. Let's have homes and offices where the best man or woman does the job most suited to their inclinations. In short, let's not only sign a peace treaty in the sex war, but ratify it too.

NO MORE FIN DE SIÈCLE, PLEASE...

Kate Mosse

I'm finding this love affair with the millennium a pain in the arse.

I wouldn't want anyone to think I'm not looking forward to the party. I am. I sit around with my children having a fantastic time working out what we might do or where we might be as the old century jumps over into the new. It goes without saying we've come to no decision yet, although fireworks will almost unavoidably be involved...

But beyond thoughts of champagne and chocolate, I do wonder if this endless obsession with time future is distracting us from the very serious business of time present. If history has taught us anything, it's that it does not respect the calendar. Significance comes through action and event, the remorseless building of layer upon layer. And although I acknowledge the symbolism of the next millennium, logically I see no reason why dreams should be realised at that arbitrary point in time or its immediate aftermath. I over-simplify, but I don't believe the world will change in the reverberating silence after the last stroke of midnight on 1 January 2000 any more than it might in January 2001, February 2002 or March 2003.

We live, now, surrounded by images of the world of the future. Where once religion and thoughts of salvation or damnation ruled people's minds, now we are blasted by visions of an over-heated planet, the spectre of woman as incubator, the fear of aggressive retroviruses that will destroy nations like an act of retribution if the biopirates or novel foods haven't finished us off first. Scientists are the new Gods, filling our newspapers and bookshelves and broadcasts with their opinions. The future is promise. The future is threat.

Culturalists are now clairvoyants too. Poets, novelists, film makers, philosophers are all trading strongly in the future. Only the traditional lyric arts of opera and ballet take their primary inspiration from the past and present. Everywhere else, where once science fiction knew its place, now it knows no boundaries. From the children's BBC series *The Demon Headmaster* to *The Handmaid's Tale*, prediction is accepted and installed in the popular market. Tomorrow is here. We are living it now.

Until a couple of years ago, the phrase 'the year 2000' still had the power to excite, conjuring up images of silver spaceships and aliens. Now, most of us have become immune to the concept of a fresh start. The millennium has lost its mystery. It's already old news. Our diaries stretch into the next century, even if our credit cards can't make it. We know that the first day of the next one thousand years will be a Saturday. Football matches will be played, children will watch cartoons in their pyjamas in the early morning, hung-over adults will swallow tea, toast and Ibuprofen to perk themselves up. Some countries will be rich, some poor. Some people will have everything they want, others nothing they need. *Plus ça change*. Time passes. It pays no attention to us.

But does it matter, this enormous burden we are placing on the inevitable? If we hitch our dreams and aspirations for the future to the millennium – rather than rooting them in something more enduring and personal – then we condemn ourselves to disappointment. A sequence of failed New Year resolutions writ large. If we wish time away in thinking of what might be – of who we could be – then surely we are guilty of wasting time?

We should dream, of course we should. We should take stock. But there is no time to lose. Starting from today, women should learn to praise themselves and take seriously their own abilities, whatever they are. No more false modesty. Too often in the past, we have shared or squandered our talents when we should have been committing ourselves to them. If that means campaigning against pollution, then great. If it means composing a symphony, great. If it means caring for children, great. Each to their own.

Writers are dreamers. Imagining what might be, improving and reordering the present. But it's easy to be lazy, easy to photograph the world rather than seek to interpret it. Too much of what is published is old-fashioned, no more than a straightforward catalogue of what exists, concerned only with gluing characters to plot. Collapsing marriages, swaggering anti-heroes, depressed wives, menopausal middle-aged men. We need more literary entrepreneurialism, less safety.

Over the past three years, as Co-Founder, Administrator (and now Honorary Director) of the Orange Prize for fiction I've read hundreds of novels by women. Some were exquisite, some provocative, some grabbed me by the throat, some moved me, some made me laugh. But other books were depressing. Similar in tone, preoccupied with the same old themes, with too little risk or debate. Perhaps this is no more than stating the obvious, a reflection on the state of the marketplace as much as the quality of ideas out there. And this tiredness is as true for novels written by men, if not more so. The majority of judges of literary prizes and bursaries I've come across claim to be disappointed, on some level, at both the lack of originality and the repetitive nature of some of the submissions. There is a tendency in British and American publishing – with certain notable exceptions including The Women's Press, Bloodaxe, Serpent's Tail, Fourth Estate – to follow a trend rather than set one. Perhaps great writers only come round once in a while and it is naive to expect anything else?

Whatever the final analysis, it's essential that female writers don't allow themselves to be lazy. There are still many people who assume that a woman writing about women is meant for women's eyes only, whereas men writing about boys is Literature. There are critics who don't believe in the power of female imagination, assuming that anything powerful is per se the result of personal experience, not creativity or skill. From the biological determinists to the young fogies reviewing for the broadsheets, the idea that genius is predominantly a male attribute still has currency.

So, I am hoping that women will raise their sights. Both as readers of fiction and as writers of it. Most readers are loyal to a small family of authors in the same way that most authors are loyal to particular ideas or styles. Thrillers, literary fiction, science fiction, fantasy, detective stories, we all have our favourites. It's easy to be attracted only to subjects that reflect our interests or values, characters we understand.

In terms of the judging and marketing of literature, the comfort of the familiar is one of the explanations for the continuing predominance of male writers on the shortlists of awards and book review pages. More often than not, like is attracted to like. And for as long as there are more men than women occupying the positions of choice then, by and large, I suspect this imbalance will persist despite the best efforts of editors, librarians and booksellers.

If women's literary imaginations are to develop, we must expand our horizons. Aim to write larger books, be less parochial. Of course some writers are miniaturists, but surely we need more Toni Morrisons and fewer Jane Austens to see us through the twenty-first century. Authors who will not shrink from imagining fantastic worlds or experimenting with style and form, authors who will pull their readers with them. We must not be humble and we must not fear failure. Instead, we should set ourselves the goal of occupying some of the space currently reserved for the BMWS – Big Male Writers.

None of us should underestimate the importance of literature over the next ten, twenty or even thirty years. Technocrats promote the importance of emerging technologies as if books were little more than relics of a slower age. In fact, whatever the mind-blowing possibilities of the science of communication, reading a novel will continue to be one of the few genuinely personal experiences. A unique contract between each individual reader and an author, different every time. We must remember this and ensure that women's imaginations and experiences and visions are really out there.

So let's dream, by all means. But dream wisely.

ALIEN

Yasmin Alibhai-Brown

I find it hard to imagine being on this planet in the twenty-first century. All the sci-fi indoctrination I have suffered over the years means I envisage an Earth full of strange creatures with funny heads and insect eyes shuffling about with too much speed for their small feet. Alternatively I imagine alienating *Mad Max* landscapes occupied only by relentless youth charging about noisily and aggressively, as if the old have finally been persuaded in the national interest to quietly put themselves to death and babies have become extinct.

Some of these nightmares are obviously to do, in a peculiar way, with how I regard my own life. It seems greedy to assume that I will have more time. Surely spanning one century should be enough for anyone of modest expectations? Make space, voices inside my head seem to say, you have done what you could and now leave it all behind. I will only just be 50 at the start of the new century. Where I come from, in Africa, for most that would be a life long enough to thank God for. These are not, I hasten to add, suicidal hallucinations or manifestations of some buried, unresolved guilt. It is something more existential. Maybe too many messages of environmental disasters and population explosions have taken their toll, eroding my optimism and aspiration.

And yet I must have some hope for the future because I have chosen to have children and I don't believe I could have done this if I truly felt that aliens were going to zap my son and daughter or that the fumes of progress would corrode their bodies and souls! So let me try and imagine then what I see for them. Let me speak as a mother, for it is as a mother that I feel most deeply fulfilled in my life, and it is this motherhood which evokes in me my greatest hopes and fears.

Ari, my son, is a young man of 20, and (truly) tall, dark and handsome. He loves the company of women and is engaging and mixed up enough to be madly interesting to them. His father and I were Ugandan Asians, rootless people who made a home here in Britain. Ari then lived through the unexpected departure of his father, the anger of a mother who still finds that hard to forgive and the reconstruction of a different family where an English stepfather had to provide much of the emotional sustenance he needed. Then, just as he was troubled and troublesome in his late teens (buying endless potions for his spots and pretending he knew all about fine wines), along came a half-sister. Leila is wild and all of four and three-quarters as I write this. People say she is ravishingly beautiful, so I often dress her down, keep her hair too short and unattractive, as if to protect her from those evil eyes and desires I feel stalk the world. Like most parents, my first wish is simply for them to survive, to be there as the next millennium unfolds and for their hearts and minds not to be destroyed by the increasing harshness I imagine will surround them.

My dread for them is boundless, some (like my statistically accurate husband) would say senseless. And it is there even when I am being unusually sensible, telling myself that the world doesn't change all that much and that it will just plod along to its own rhythm, barely noticing these artificial timelines. I still worry. Will Ari be able to abide this strangely distancing country without wanting to wreak havoc either inside himself or out there? He thinks of himself as British, deeply so. I never have and cannot now. He is, I know, too uppity for the place reserved for him as an Asian man. We are (supposedly) those diligent ones, who still too often bow our heads and praise our past and present lords, busying ourselves obligingly in those indispensable corner shops and pharmacies. Our children are finding this increasingly difficult, my son particularly so. I worry about the consequences of this. Will he be arrested one day for no good reason, starting the downward spiral where his broken faith ends up destroying that proud self I have so carefully nurtured?

Maybe these are unnecessary anxieties. Maybe Ari, being so strong and bold and clever, and so tuned now to the winning ways of the metropolitan middle classes, will turn himself into the Mandelson of the 2020s, when he should be just the right age. But if this happens, will his talents be appropriated and his identity compromised, locking him out for ever from his ancestral roots? Will there be anything left then of my gifts to him – his always protesting and fighting black/Asian mother?

Maybe it is often the case that children reject the ways of their parents, and perhaps Ari will extend this to the philosophical and cultural spheres. He will perhaps conform and belong, never glancing in the direction of any of the things that keep me grounded and excluded: listening to sad Hindi songs, eating my food with my hands, seeking the comfort of my four home languages, not counting English. Perhaps the whole world will have surrendered itself to the hegemonic power of the West by then and only museums will remember, and show on small screens, how those from afar who came to stay, surreptitiously ate dhal and rice with their hands, beautifully, delicately, and with such humility as they caressed the food instead of attacking it with stainless steel weapons. Ari squirms when he watches me do any of the above, so his point of cultural identity, his national pride are clearly rooted here in Britain.

And then there is Leila, half pukkah English, who is already coming home to say that she will not play with that child Hassan in her school because he is 'too dark brown'. I panic at this and tell her she is half-Asian much too often, in the vain hope that she will cling to that 'brown' side of hers – threatened as it already is. And I hope that maybe now that I am older and bolder than I was when my son was born, I can teach her the languages, the pride; her core enlarged by her father's history and also mine. I no longer feel that burdensome urge to please my white masters or to shave off bits of myself they find alien. Maybe I can help her understand her 'too dark brown' side better, this time round.

But perhaps this will be impossible. Even if I do manage to sneak into the next century for a few years, I know God will have taken my own mother well before the next decade is through. She is my only true link with my heritage. It is with her and through her that I keep those parts going. As that generation disappears, all our languages – Kutchi (with its lovely cadences and concepts uncontaminated by modernity), Gujarati, Hindi and Swahili – will have been starved out of existence. Some call it cultural genocide, I prefer to call it cultural neglect by a state that has never let them thrive within its educational system. No one in this country will say things like 'my soul can't breathe today' or 'think, do and see' the way we can in our languages. And when a language disappears, you lose the key to that culture. This now seems inevitable.

*

In other ways too what I hope for is clouded by fear. Will we, can we, halt the terrifying descent into moral anarchy? I grew up in an atmosphere of hothouse morality. Retribution, obligation, selflessness, dominated my every action from the time I could understand such things. And while such morality can be restrictive, it seems to me there is a need for a more ethical value system than currently exists. My hope is that we will create something solid that replaces moral authoritarianism on the one hand and moral anarchy on the other, realigning the balance between freedom of the individual and the needs of family, community and society. It is depressing to feel that there is such a priority given to individual freedom that other more collective, communal rights and responsibilities, can now only be seen as oppressive and limiting, rather than potentially liberating and beneficial. A recent survey shows that women are less happy in their marriages than men are. Other research reveals that it is women who most often initiate divorce. This is not something to celebrate. We have to find new ways of living and loving for the twenty-first century. And for women in heterosexual relationships, this means, of course, men will have to change. Already many men – not most – have made great shifts, and I love them for it. I hope my son and daughter find comfort and joy in their relationships, and that they will feel enough faith to have children of their own.

Behind these fears there are others, more complex. As a Muslim woman who has moved closer to her faith in the past few years, what can I look forward to as I look to the future? I despair and ache as I watch the grotesque spectacle of the Taliban extinguishing all signs of life in the women of Afghanistan, supported as ever by Western money. There our youngest and brightest don their hijabs and blindly support the insupportable, because they are that dislocated and disenchanted with the West. The Islam that will survive will not be the Islam I grew up with, where truth, aesthetics, love and sensuality were a part of what God had given us to use and enjoy. How will my children ever understand that heritage, and who will blame them if they remove all signs of this religion from their lives?

So these then are my imaginings. A Britain where my children are supposedly free to be themselves, but where they will not fight against the cultural norms. I will watch from wherever I am, and possibly I will weep because there will be nobody left to challenge the view that the West knows best. That this is the apex of human achievement, the final destination of human endeavour. Colonialism went a long way in destroying non-Western people, their cultures and self-expression, even attempting to obliterate their histories. But the project was left incomplete. When the empire came home, however, the final resolution became possible as our cultures were borrowed and assimilated. As the iconoclastic writer Ziauddin Sardar wrote in the terrible aftermath of the Rushdie affair: 'Secularism, in its post-modernist phase of desperate self glorification has embarked on this goal.'[1] Ashis Nandy, a brilliant Indian writer and philosopher, develops this theme and warns of the dangers if we all throw ourselves into this melting cauldron:

> Many non-observers view of the modern West – its lifestyle, literature, arts, and its human sciences – have been struck by the way contractual competitive individualism – and the utter loneliness that flows from it – dominates the

> Western mass society. From Friedrich Nietzsche to Karl Marx to Franz Kafka, much of Western social analysis too has stood witness to this cultural pathology. What once looks like independence from one's immediate authority in the family and defiance of the larger aggregates they represented, now looks like a Hobbesian worldview gone rabid.[2]

This, combined with a massively controlled and manipulated population who have to be told what to wear or eat, how they may make love, which cars they must buy and how to decorate their homes, means that as I look down or peer up at the world after I have departed – what will probably be most striking is that people are all the same. The only hope is that your children fight against it, and mine too. But being caught so early and processed so mercilessly will they be able to fight? I am not sure...

Notes

1 Ziauddin Sardar, *Distorted Imagination*, Grey Seal, 1990, p276.

2 Ashis Nandy, 'Cultural Frames for Social Transformation', in *Alternatives*, vol 12:1, 1987.

A LIFE IN A DAY

Shelley Bovey

In my book The Forbidden Body: Why Being Fat Is Not a Sin, *I wrote an imaginary, though all too real piece called* 'A Day in the Life of a Fat Woman'. *Set as it was in the context of the prevailing anti-fat climate, it struck deep chords with many women who had experienced and identified with the harsh realities of a world where no accommodation was made for size and fat women in particular were outlawed. The following is a day with an altogether different emphasis: a utopian view that we can attain if we keep the faith and keep working towards such a change.*

Seven a.m. on an early spring morning and the sunrise is pink in the gaps between the rooftops. The woman stretches and smiles, coming languidly awake as her clock radio greets her with a nostalgic ballad from the nineties.

She turns on to her back and runs her hands over the curves of her body under the nightshirt. Her hips are wide and soft, made for swaying and for dancing, for love and for childbirth, for the rhythms of life. There is no sharp jut of pelvic bones. Her belly rises making a mound under the quilt, full as it once was with child but soft now, not taut as it had been then. She circles it with her arms, lifting it, enjoying its fluid movement. Her breasts are a law unto themselves; they lie where they will, not standing pert and upright like those of a thin woman. They follow the laws of gravity.

She dresses, choosing her clothes for spring, for celebration.

She spends a lot on them, she knows, but how can she resist when what is available is so glorious? When colours and fabrics and fashions of all kinds call her from store after store? Fashion victim, she chides herself, laughing.

Downstairs she makes her breakfast. Muesli, rich with fruit and nuts and honey. Creamy yoghurt to top it and then apricot toast with butter. There had been a time when she was younger when her breakfast had consisted of a small glass of fruit juice and one very thin slice of bread with a scraping of vile-tasting spread out of a plastic box. They didn't make that now. It was supposed to help people keep slim but some said it had contained carcinogenic trans-fats. Thank goodness the days of deprivation were over. She used to be hungry, tired, obsessed with food, forever on a yo-yo between weight loss and gain. She was glad her own daughter had grown up in an era when so-called reducing diets were an anachronism.

It is time to drive to the station to catch the London train. She had taken delivery of her new car the day before and is looking forward to trying it out. The man at the garage had taken a lot of care in adjusting the position of the steering wheel so that it did not dig into her stomach. This facility was standard on all cars, as was the choice of seat belt length. After all, people came in all shapes and sizes; they were not all expected to fit the same dimensions. Time was, she remembered, when she could not do up a car seat belt without it cutting into her throat because it was too short to reach over the swell of her belly and breasts. Should an accident occur, she would have had to choose between the prospect of death by strangulation as the seat belt locked, or by grave injury from being precipitated through the windscreen.

The new design trains are a pleasure to travel on. Seats are much larger and there are far fewer than on the old-style trains. Aisles are wider, comfort is greater all round. She chooses a large, single seat and settles herself for the journey. It was not always like this: she is old enough to remember years past when there were tables only a few inches from the seats and they were not easy to negotiate, even for thin people. She used to face a journey with hot dread, pulling in as much of herself as she could, pushing her body into the seat, jammed for a few agonising moments as her stomach caught on the hard rim of the table. She never went to the buffet car on a long journey; she could not bear to repeat the performance. In those days, others were not kind to people like her and any manoeuvre was watched with harsh judgement, with annoyance, sniggers or hateful remarks.

At the London terminus she heads for the underground. Slipping easily through a turnstile she dashes for the train she can hear approaching. As she runs, moving with grace and ease, she attracts admiring glances. She recognises them for what they are: she has no false modesty and she smiles in return. The tube trains of this century have also undergone transformation; here, too, seats are broad and comfortable, and although strap-hanging is not allowed it is not needed for there are plenty of trains.

She chats with her neighbour, remembering the time when she would sit, desperately trying not to take up more than her share of the space available, wrapping her arms around herself to pull her shoulders in, squeezing her legs together tightly, trying not to spill over into her neighbour's seat. People would glare and make remarks about her size that were often audible and which brought tears of humiliation to her eyes. Living in the twentieth century had not been quite the nightmare Orwell had portrayed in *1984*, but for fat people it was just as much of a dystopia.

She arrives at her office in the heart of London; she is the travel editor of a popular mainstream women's magazine. Most of her colleagues are women and as usual the talk turns to looks. She despairs of this preoccupation but is resigned; it was ever thus. Gaia, her assistant, is depressed. She is in the fourth week of yet another diet and it doesn't seem to be working. She is genetically predisposed to be thin, so increasing her intake of food just won't do the trick. 'You're so lucky,' Gaia moans. 'I'd give anything for a figure like yours.'

She tries to reassure her unhappy colleague but knows it will be of little help: women hell-bent on dieting have tunnel vision. 'You are beautiful as you are,' she tells Gaia. 'Look at all the icons of the twentieth century – Kate Moss, Joanna Lumley, Princess Diana. They were all thin. Besides, isn't it what's inside that really counts?'

'It should be,' agrees Gaia, with a sigh. 'But social pressure is so great and it's even worse working in the media as we do. It's hard to believe that women actually used to starve themselves to *lose* weight.' She sympathises with Gaia, remembering how it was when she was outcast for being fat, before the cultural tide turned. Gaia tells her that her doctor has prescribed a diet pill called Wate-Gain. There are risky side effects but she says she feels desperate. 'I want to wear decent clothes,' she says. 'But there's nothing stylish below a size fourteen.'

Later she has lunch with the editor and two of the magazine's writers. Mealtimes are important social occasions where the sharing of delicious, health-giving food is a symbol and a celebration of common humanity, of life, of abundance. People do not pick at their food unless they are ill but eat with a sensuality and gusto that used to be untypical of the British. There is no shame or guilt around eating, and the consequences of this are that people are in touch with all their appetites, at home with their sexual natures which are so closely allied to the enjoyment of food and of flesh. She learned, long ago, that to feed herself with enough goodness, enough delights, caused the body to regulate itself. When deprivation is not a constantly lurking self-inflicted punishment, the craving for excess does not occur. She relishes the combination of good food and good company and the lunch is an enjoyable satisfaction of all the senses.

When she was a young woman, just starting her career, she had not dared to order anything but 'diet' food at working lunches, aware of the censorious eyes of her editor. One day she had been particularly hungry and unable to resist salmon *en croûte*. The magazine editor, staring at her disdainfully while eating her own small salad, had not commented on her choice of 'sinful' food. Instead she had suggested a diet feature, a before-and-after makeover piece. 'We could do a lot with you,' she had said. 'Such a pretty face – it's a shame you're so overweight.' A direct hit, one that hurt.

She does not return to the office for the afternoon. She has a hospital appointment for a Well Woman check. Despite the advances of medical science, a number of things can go wrong at her age, some years post-menopause, and regular checks are a wise precaution.

She is asked to undress and to put on a gown. She recalls the hospital appointments of her youth, of her childbearing years, humiliating obstetrical examinations of a time when medical staff were unstintingly rude to women of her size. They had threatened her with everything from refusals to perform operations to the certainty of poor health and early death. She remembers the embarrassment of standing in X-ray departments, half-naked under gowns that would not meet round her body, trying in vain to hold on to her dignity. Thin may not be fashionable now, and thin women have long since fallen out of favour as cultural icons, but they are not persecuted as once the fat had been.

Now she selects a roomy robe from a number of different sizes and makes her way to an examination room. A doctor and a nurse perform a full-body scan, a routine and safe procedure that has replaced the inelegant mammograms and uncomfortable smear tests of the past. It takes very little time and they are able to tell her at once that she is in excellent health. Nowadays a scan can measure all the body's functions, obviating the necessity of old-style ECGs or blood pressure readings. A written analysis of the scan will follow to confirm the findings.

There are questions she wants to ask. Because she is over 60 and because she has never quite shaken off the painful experiences of the anti-fat indoctrination of her youth, she wants to know the health implications of her size. 'Your fitness level is superb,' the doctor tells her. 'Why the concern about your weight?'

'Won't there come a point,' she asks a little anxiously, 'when it will put a strain on my heart?'

The doctor understands. 'That's what they told you when you were much younger? They believed then that high weight inevitably led to all manner of disease and death, but research has long since proved that was complete fallacy.' She knows this, of course. She's read the research, but a little reassurance does not go amiss. 'The trouble was that the late twentieth-century lifestyle was pretty unhealthy,' the doctor continues. 'High fat food and not enough exercise did enormous harm. They made fat people scapegoats because the medical profession was particularly prejudiced. We know now that good lifestyle factors and a stable weight are predictors of longevity. You are absolutely fine and I would be surprised if you didn't make it to 95.'

Before she goes home she spends an enjoyable and relaxing hour in the swimming pool in the centre of her office complex. She shops for ingredients for supper, lingering over succulent organic fruit and vegetables, fresh fish, lean meat and scrumptious pastries. She has friends coming for supper and cooking is a joy.

She dozes in her comfortable seat on the train home, looking forward to the next day...and the next, and the next.

Life is good for a fat woman in the first half of the twenty-first century.

AN UNSHARED CENTURY

Anees Jung

Another monsoon has passed. This one my mother has only sensed, not seen. She now knows the rains when the earth turns fresh and fragrant. Having been witness to ninety glorious monsoons my mother has turned blind. The darkness that circles her life seems to be the toll she is paying for having known the light of nearly a century, a light she saw but never went out and reached.

Like the rains. She never stood in the fields with the peasants scanning the sky, praying for the dark clouds to roll in, for the rain to fall and quench the blazing earth, the wilting trees. She watched them from the windows of the house her father owned with its miles of paddy fields and thousands of tamarind trees. When the rains failed she watched the fields recede. They sulked, turned brown and withered. Like the people who worked on them. They shrank and died without food in the famines that followed. Famines and storms were the events that marked her childhood years, though they never crossed her father's 'dahleej', the three crucial stone steps that separated the house from the world outside.

The most momentous event in the ninety years of my mother's life was at the dawn of the century when Hyderabad, the city of her birth, was caught in the eye of a storm. It was a black night at the end of the days of the moon. The river Musi had risen high enough to drown an elephant. Like an ocean its waters billowed, surged over roofs, swept away bridges, trees, people. The waves rose from the river bed and lapped on the doorsteps of the houses that lined its banks. In one such house was my grandmother, nursing a girl 40 days old. To save her from the river's wrath, my grandmother went around the house with a piece of charcoal writing the name of Allah on the walls so that they would not be washed away. The walls stood, as did the faith of a simple, God-fearing woman. The girl survived, hearing each year the story of the miracle that saved the house and her life.

No other storm holds a similar significance for my mother. Not even the political storm that swept across the country and encircled her state, threatening its treasured autonomous identity. It was 1947, the year of India's independence from the British. Beyond her high white walls raged the historic police action that was to change the destiny of Hyderabad, making it a part of the Indian Union. She was nearly forty, a mother of five children. Her husband, deeply involved in the events of the time, never talked to her about politics. The city fell. The Nizam whom the British had blessed with the title of His Exalted Highness, whom she reverently referred to as 'Huzoor', turned into an ordinary citizen. The city of Hyderabad slipped from its life of regal splendour into being one of 17 states of the Indian Union without my mother knowing it. The people of her beloved state, bowed by centuries of feudal rule, were technically free. My mother did not know it. Her own courtyard, green with trees of mango and lemon, fragrant with jasmines and roses, continued to enclose her life, shielding it from any visible storm, natural, political or personal.

The first crack in the white walls appeared one autumnal night when my father died suddenly. People swarmed into the house for his funeral. The world entered her home. Through the fine cane curtain of her room she watched the crowd darkly, shrank away in horror when she saw a man, presumably her husband's friend, walk away with his platinum pocket watch. She remained silent. Her young children crowded around her in a weak effort to guard and protect. Today she continues to live in their shadow, the same way she did, first with her father, then her husband. It is her daughters who nurture and support her and their shadows are smaller, seemingly less durable. The men in her life have disappeared. The two sons have gone into their own lives. She laments their withdrawal, deems it unfortunate, unnatural. For tradition demands that a son not a daughter must provide the shade for a mother.

Is it my mother's final journey, I wonder, as I escort her back to Hyderabad, the city that has stayed static in her dreams. She left it soon after her husband's death, followed the children to bigger cities as they each pursued a separate dream. Their world began crowding into hers without really changing it. To this day my mother has not stepped out on her own. She has not been inside a bank for she has never possessed money of her own; she has never gone shopping, never sat in a restaurant and eaten a meal by herself or gone out on a walk to experience a sunset on her own. A daughter is always around, interpreting the passing scenes of the outside world from the windows of fast-moving cars. But her interest in the outside has been awakened. She has begun to see with the eyes of her growing children. She listens to them attentively and, when alone, to the radio. What she hears she discusses with them the way a child would who is excited with the new explorations.

She is intrigued, often fascinated, by the stories I tell her – of countries she has not visited, of friends I have made, many of them men. She raises no objections though she never knew any men in her life, except her husband. My mother has no friends except her children. She has had no one to share her private thoughts or fears with. They remain locked in her and will go with her to the grave. I have glimpses of her anguish while reading the poems she has written for years and hidden away. When I found them hidden between newspapers and old books I sought her permission and had them published. She was ecstatic to see them compiled in a book which she knew others would read. But when I insisted that the book be sold she was embarrassed. Her poems were her private world which no one should be allowed to purchase or visit. She does not object though to the fact that my books are sold, that I bare my thoughts every week in newspapers, letting countless readers enter my mind and heart, even my soul.

She knows that I live in a century that has lost its privacy. She also knows that I am more alone than she is, even in her darkness. My life has followed a route diametrically opposed to hers. I have lived life always on my own terms. I have travelled the world, almost always alone. I have sat by myself in cafés, relished my meals, befriended strangers. I have lived for years in an apartment with no other company except my own. And I have gone to bed with a mind crowded, alone.

Through the years this 'aloneness' has acquired a celebratory tone. It is a solitude that has helped me define myself, provided me with a strength that has given me a sense of liberation, which others sometimes find difficult to understand.

'Haven't seen you for a long time,' says a woman in the park whom I frequently encounter. 'Is everyone well at home?'

'There is no one at home,' I say, hearing my own words.

'I am so sorry,' she says, looking at me with eyes that betray pity.

'You have no reason to be,' I quip. 'I am very happy. I have travelled and experienced a big wide world. I have made a name for myself. I have friends everywhere.' Do I have to defend myself thus to a total stranger I wonder, even as I speak. Why should a woman whom I see only briefly every morning have the power to make me feel sorry for myself?

'All that is fine,' she breaks into my fears. 'So you have conquered the world! Why don't you now try and conquer the world of a home?'

Her words pursue me through the winding green, stay with me all day in the silence of my home, acquire a sinister echo in the darkness of the night. I switch on the radio to chase away the discomfort that I cannot name. A play is being broadcast, about women who lived a century ago in feudal Bengal. It is based on a classic story by the renowned writer, Sarat Chandra Chatterjee. Two women are on air, daughters-in-law of a large middle-class family. 'Why have you left the comforts of a royal home and come into this house?' asks the younger daughter-in-law. 'You, who had servants at your command, now reduced to the status of a servant in the family of the man to whom you are wedded.'

'"Ghar-grahasti" is the ultimate penance for a woman,' replies the older woman. 'To live in a family of such diverse people, and help bring that fine balance and harmony is a definitive test for women. If she succeeds she finds her bliss, her peace and salvation.'

Hearing Sarat Chandra Chatterjee's women on the radio, a hundred years after the words were first written, reminds me of my own encounter with the woman in the park who advised me to conquer the world of a home. How have a hundred years changed the hidden psyche of the Indian woman?

'I have nearly lived a century and not participated in it. You have,' says my mother. In her words I find my freedom, my redemption. For she has been a witness to my life, silently shared its struggle, its constant pains, its fleeting joys. Like many women of her generation my mother was not groomed to struggle for a life of her own. In the youth of her century, to be ambitious, even for one's own personal happiness, was considered bad form. To negate one's desire (that was often anyway only seen as greed), to sacrifice for a larger peace, to guard one's honour and that of the family, was a condition which she was born to and in which she has lived. Her identity has been preserved only within the confines of her family, extending at times to a slightly larger clan within a community. She has not found reason to question or demystify it. Like the women in Sarat Chandra Chatterjee's stories in feudal Bengal. Like the woman in the Delhi park who jogs every morning draped so guardedly in a six-yard sari. But unlike them she has begun to question. She is aware that she has not participated in this century, that it has slipped by her, without her learning the right to claim it.

A NEW WOODLAND: CREATING WOMEN'S LAND FOR THE FUTURE

Caeia March

The concept of women's land is hundreds of years old. Throughout the history of the earth, women have lived and worked side by side in women-only communities: as far apart in time and space as ancient China, Sapphic Lesbos, the Beguines of twelfth- to fourteenth-century Europe, and the matriarchal/matrifocal societies of Africa, India and the Americas.

Why, then, have I and other women opted for a tiny, two-acre project in the 'toe' of Britain in the second half of the twentieth century? Because it is all we have! As one of the founding mothers of our project has said, 'There are two acres of men's land in every village in England, the cricket pitch and the football field, so it is not going over the top to have two acres for women in the whole of Cornwall, is it?'

The vision of the Beguine women, who lived on the land in communities near to the hospitals and poor houses of the major cities of Europe, was very real to me following my research for my novel, *Between the Worlds*. I wanted something similar. I had also visited several different areas of women's land in the USA and for many years longed to be part of a rural community of women, planting trees and herbs, growing food and working on the land together. Women respond to land in many different and creative ways, by painting, singing, making music and dancing. I hope to use my love of the written word to convey the magic of our women's land in Cornwall and what it means to me at this time, which is Lughnasad, the festival of the beginning of harvest, at the end of the twentieth century.

I first visited women's land in Cornwall in December 1987. It belonged to a woman potter who loved the Goddess and had a visionary approach to sacred space and women's space. It had been much loved by women from Greenham, for whom it had provided a sanctuary away from the conflict and confrontation there – a place to be renewed and refreshed for the next stage of the struggle to free Greenham Common from nuclear weapons. I fell in love with the place which consisted of converted barns and three acres of fields, one of which had been planted as sacred woodland with a circle of baby oaks and alders, for ritual purposes.

In 1992 I moved into the barns on the land as a tenant and lived there on and off till 1994. Sadly, that land had to be sold but this led four of us – my partner Cheryl Straffon and I and two other women – to fundraise for a new women's land. We achieved this, buying the two acres which are now held in trust for all women for all time.

The fundraising was amazing – a very exciting time. Money came in in donations from five pounds upwards, and from all over England, Wales, Scotland – and abroad too. We had to find four thousand pounds for the two acres and three hundred for solicitors' fees. Later we continued to fundraise to get a water connection into the mains that, miraculously, ran under the land by the eastern boundary, and for some sensitive JCB work to clear some 'swales' in which to plant the baby trees.

When I stand on this new land, surrounded by a ring of sacred hills – Bartinney, which was one of the twin holy hilltops on which fires were lit at summer solstice, Caer Bran with its ancient fort, and

Sancreed Beacon with its burial chambers – I feel a deep connection with ancestral spirits and I have a keen sense of women's lives stretching back thousands of years. I know that here on these hills women gathered firewood and sought out healing herbs. I know that hereabouts they raised their children and sang to the moon and took part in many acts of ritual at the festivals which marked the turn of the agricultural year. I know this not from any airy-fairy new-age dreaming but from archaelogical evidence of the use of the landscape all around this area, including for example, Carn Euny ancient settlement.

Carn Euny is known as a courtyard house settlement and includes a beehive hut with a circular corbelled room; a fogou, which is a human-made underground passage or cave for ritual purposes, and several visible but ruined circular hut dwellings. Also, about a quarter of a mile away, either side of a footpath at the base of the hill of Bartinney, there is a pair of holy wells, one of which is approached by seven granite steps leading into the ground. There under a lintel the clear water flows, leaving the well to become the Lamorna stream on its way to the sea. There on each of the first three Wednesdays in May, women would bring their sick children for healing. The children would be dipped three times into the well then carried widdershins (against the sun) three times around the well, and this triple three ceremony continued from the ancient past into the twentieth century. Knowing the healing history of this area adds a special poignancy to the location of the women's land as we approach the twenty-first century. It gives a sense of continuity of vision and purpose, and a powerful feeling of communication across time and space with the women of past and future millennia.

*

When we first purchased the land, it was a bare field which had been set to pasture and was fringed by high Cornish hedges of foxgloves, primroses, pink campions and hawthorn trees. Today, two years later, the central area is a wild flower grassy space, and the edges have a swathe of newly planted baby trees in order to create a shelter belt.

The western edge has two sacred circles, created by flattening the land and planting trees – cherry around one circle and hazel around the other. They can be used for individual or group meditation, for connection with the land, the earth, and the spirits of place. The eastern edge has three larger flat circles. One has a fire pit around which it is possible for women to dance, and it may be decided that the other two will be encircled by living huts created by planting willows and other 'bendy trees' that can be shaped to provide privacy and peace.

Forty or so women have come from local towns and villages and some from as far away as St Austell, Bristol, Bradford and Brighton to plant the trees, which were provided under the Cornish tree planting scheme. Shortly after we purchased the land, we held a site meeting with a representative from the local council who was able to advise us as to the best trees to plant for the first round of planting. It was pointed out that the elevation of the land was at the upper limit of the natural 'tree line', above which the land would lend itself best to moorland varieties of low growing heather and ling, with some gorse. The land is highest in the south, so along the southern boundary we chose a mixture of young hawthorn and blackthorn, which can withstand the wind and salt in the air. The sloping western boundary was chosen for a mixed planting of grey alder, common alder, and grey willow, and along the northern edge, at the bottom of the land, a similar mix was interspersed with elder, and a few specimens of maritime pine and larch.

Many individual women have helped with the different kinds of work. Firstly the baby trees really need our input. They have to be weeded and cared for continuously, for this is not an easy place for them to begin their long lives – the site is sloping and is windy at all times of the year and can be very exposed in winter. They are young and vulnerable, and the more care that they get in their early years, the more joy and abundance they can give back as they grow. They will provide a shelter belt for the other activities, privacy for all of us, and a delight and sustenance to the birds and creatures who will come to live on the land and in the new woodland.

Other land work includes brambling and maintenance of the hedgerows, and the clearance of dock and thistles from the central wild flower meadow. We are fortunate that the land has not been polluted by chemicals for several years – the wild flowers are already beginning to return. Several of us had a hilariously dirty time making the concrete base for the ten by eight shed, which now stands in the north-eastern corner, and for most of us concreting was a new skill. We laughed a great deal during the process, because it was like making a large, substantial cake – with a careful weighing of ingredients and a heavy-duty cake mixer. We used five buckets of aggregate to one of dry cement, kept the mixer going continuously, added water to the right consistency and hey presto. Nothing to it – not when you've been cooking for years! As usual we took photos for the archive, though we couldn't be identified under all the layers of grime. Later we concreted the two gateposts for the huge farm gate which marks the south-west entrance for vehicular access. When the JCB work was being done, we asked for a smaller entrance at the bottom of the land, which will eventually have a wooden disabled access walkway.

Not everyone can get to the land easily or regularly, but that doesn't matter. All the land work takes time, and every separate hour of input makes this project happen. If one woman can nurture one tree, or care for one square metre of land, then it helps to keep this dream alive and to make it, day by day, into a reality to take us forward together. Each one of the thousand trees needs us, and even a few minutes of input can give a tree a chance to grow and someone, somewhere, a chance to heal.

The other key area of work is communication and networking – telling other women, everywhere, about the land, sharing the dream and the excitement of the project, which is a lifelong commitment for many of us. Some women will feel inclined to become trustees by attending regular meetings on and for the land, helping to take decisions and to create new plans and activities. Some of our future plans include a witches' herb garden, an orchard of native apples, and a scented garden for the blind.

In the first year the trustees developed a constitution and set of aims. This involved some long, tedious and exhausting meetings but this was all more than worthwhile for it allowed us, among other things, to apply for and obtain funding for a shed and materials for a shed base, a seat for disabled women, tools for planting trees, and an industrial-weight strimmer for major clearance work. Alongside this were many fundraising activities including jumble sales and sponsored swims, and even haircuts.

For the future, I would hope that new areas of women's land could be purchased in different parts of Britain (as is already happening, for example, on the Isle of Lewis), so that city women do not have far to travel to take part in tending the land and planting trees. In effect, we have created a 'millennium' wood in Cornwall – what a wonderful thing to have done for future generations of women to enjoy. The thousand baby trees are but a beginning – I would like to see many areas of deforested hills and valleys replanted with native species. I would also hope for some camping facilities especially for women, and some residential projects, but these would cost so much more money and the issues of tenants/caretakers are difficult to resolve, especially in terms of continuity of use. Quiet spaces, areas of safety for meditation and relaxation are really needed by women. To have been part of creating one such haven, albeit a tiny one, feels wonderful, and a great privilege.

I personally experience this land as sacred – a wonderful haven, a lovely place of peacefulness on mother earth. And we have found that very many women have a delighted response to this land. Women who are not actively seeking a spiritual path come here, and then find that they can and do connect with the earth as a sanctuary of safety and beauty, where 'mother nature' reveals herself to all her daughters, in so many different ways. For me, I feel a sense of harvest in a very specific way – the harvesting of the original dream. I experience this land and this project as a way to give something back to the earth mother, to return to her that which is truly hers – her flowers, her trees, her hedgerows, her wild grasses, and the creatures who once again can come to live therein. I feel that I have learned from some of the earlier tensions and meetings – to not be in so much of a hurry, to let things grow more slowly, more organically perhaps, and that includes the group work of the role of the trustees. Trustees are the guardians of the land, and it is the land herself who can teach us what to do, and the best ways to work with one another to bring about the changes. The greatest feeling of all as we reach the twenty-first century is that of celebration – that if we dream this land into being, we can make this dream come true. For me, this is one way I can positively and actively give of my time, my work and my love, recognising that the earth is our mother; we must take care of her.

WOMEN WORRYING IN THE USA

Judith Arcana

Since you ask, I'll happily tell you that I am indeed proud of what women have accomplished all over the world in the twentieth century, but I have no hope for the future. I see no way that the global juggernaut of greed, made immeasurably more powerful by systems and technologies that denature their users along with their victims, can be stopped by women's movement or any other righteous movement – all of which is now informed by the revolutionary history of women.

Nevertheless, I believe we must resist that juggernaut – not because I think we will prevail, but because if we do not resist, we condemn ourselves to live in apathy, cynicism or despair, with no joy – or even authenticity – in our lives.

In support of resistance in a life committed to authenticity and opportunities for joy despite hopelessness, I urge a pragmatic willingness to accept what I think of as worrying: worrying as an accepted, expected and necessary aspect of life, worrying about what we now commonly call the 'quality of life' in a world largely dominated by ignorance, corruption, exploitation, torture and violent death.

We worry while we support and work for causes and purposes that liberate and comfort, causes and purposes that serve what we believe is justice. We worry as the fire at the heart of the world burns toward a cold so profound we cannot begin to imagine it.

Annie worries about historical evidence suggesting that no revolution has ever actually succeeded, so there's no reason for hope, no reason at all to be hopeful.

Barbara worries because now that everybody moves so often maybe it is true that we can't go home again, and she thinks this is a problem because then what is home anyway, and after all, isn't home where you're supposed to go again and again, over and over, always?

Chitra worries because so many people believe the USA is one country; they can't see that this place could never be just one thing; she thinks this is because the sprawling interstate highway system makes Atlanta look like Kansas City from the freeway exits – despite the fact that Atlanta and Kansas City are as different as Newark and El Paso.

Darneice worries because, although she had always known that there was something basically wrong with banks and the stock market, now that she's got enough money to buy a house and learn about mortgage law, she understands the connection between government and business, and she is frightened.

Elena worries about the children, because so few – incredibly few – adults have any idea at all about how to behave around them, how to treat them, what to do with and for them; Elena worries so much that she can no longer go into supermarkets, playgrounds, circuses or the beach in summertime; she can't even go into convenience stores, because always, everywhere, the grown-ups are hurting children, hitting them or making them tell lies, be quiet, be still, be ashamed.

Francine worries that she and her partner will break up, that what they wanted and needed from each other has played out like a Colorado silver mine; then they'll have to sell the house, she can't afford to keep it alone and her partner won't want it, and she'll have to move, and what if she winds up living in a carton under a railroad bridge?

Graciela worries about what the world will be like when there are no wild animals at all, no animals outside of zoos, preserves and domestication, no animals in existence who have ever lived without interference in their homes, their food, their reproduction.

Hannah worries, since racism is still so fiercely powerful in the life of the nation, that people will believe all the courage and pain of past decades has somehow gone to waste, which is, she insists, simply not true.

Isabel worries about her father and the other old people who are not rich; since there is no real system that holds them dear or even helps them be comfortable, they are tormented and humiliated in huge and tiny ways every day of their delicate grey lives.

Judy worries about the extent to which the dreadful, stupid policies of the Israeli government create and exacerbate anti-Semitism, because people are outraged when they do horrific things to Palestinian children or college students or even young men, who are the least sympathetic group everywhere in the world according to research.

Kaneesha worries about the hypocrisy of everyday personal interaction in the industrialised nations, the state of human relationships in advanced capitalism, the loss of true mythology and the rise of canned spirituality, the employment of shamanic healers by corporations, the probable construction of sweat lodges at Holiday Inns.

Lenore worries about lesbians, and gay men too – actually she worries about all the people everybody else thinks are odd – because the human capacity for evil, for pure meanness, is intensified by ignorance, and the majority of the people in the world are, she has recently begun to understand, far more ignorant than she ever realised.

Mei Mei worries about reproductive biotechnology – the making of people in petri dishes, to specifications that somebody (*who? that's a terrifying question, right? who's in charge? she wants to know, and then realises – here's where the terror comes in – that she knows very well who's in charge*) has decided are what the world needs in the way of human beings.

Naomi worries about the degradation of language, the loss of language as music and art, its rhythm so long a source of excitement and comfort for the human spirit.

Odessa worries because so many angry little countries have chemical weapons – old nerve gases and new neuropoisons – and some of them, she is sure, will be no less hesitant to use them than the big countries that like to pretend they don't make them or sell them or store them any more.

Polly worries about the rising power of those people who say women have to keep making babies, keep on making babies no matter what, even though these babies will have to grow up in poison – I mean, she says, if the air is poison, the water is poison, the soil is poison and none of this poison is going away, then why do they want us to make babies? and what about, she wonders, the fact that those very same people are not so enthusiastic about many of the babies who are already here?

Queenie worries about all the recent college graduates who take jobs with multinational corporations and ad agencies; she knows they don't see how dreadful this is, because their generation grew up thinking that anything is, like, okay, as long as it looks cool.

Rose Girl worries because people sit so long in front of computer screens, holding their hands and eyes and necks and shoulders stiffly; she thinks they'll all get sick, and she'll need physical therapy before she's twenty.

Sandy worries about her job at the fish plant disappearing and not being able to find another one when she's too old to wait tables or turn tricks like her sister in Pasadena who got kicked off welfare before her kids were old enough for school and there was a waiting list at the daycare and no family in town anymore to leave them with.

Tammy worries about how the dinosaurs disappeared, like is it true that a meteor hit where they lived, or was it that the weather changed and they died of thirst or starvation or froze to death? and isn't this important because maybe there is some connection, like they say on the public television station, between all of that and all of this, when you look at how the weather is changing, and the scientists say global warming is coming faster so its effects will be experienced in her lifetime, not safely later when her own foreseeable descendants will all be dead.

Ursula worries because almost everything she grew up with has disappeared – small-sized GrapeNuts, alarm clocks that tick, record players, running boards, and people who say that things they like a lot are *neat.*

Violet worries because she can't help thinking class and money will never be understood in a country that pretends the first doesn't exist and the second is available to everyone despite all the evidence – none of it hidden – to the contrary.

Wanda worries about the damn government lying all the time, saying there isn't enough oil, there isn't enough food, making up stories about how the so-called market forces make everything cost a lot – but she knows there's really enough, enough so they could give it away, but they won't because then big business wouldn't make big profit.

Xenia worries about how, even though some people have bumper stickers that say KILL YOUR TELEVISION – she'd definitely get one if she had a car – TV is in everybody's heads; even her own friends are talking about characters in situation comedies and soap operas like they're real, believing what they hear on the news, thinking people who don't watch TV are weird.

Yvonne worries about the youth – how they never seem to have learned anything from history, neither from the apparent facts of it nor from the experiences of those who lived in it – and how they are so absolutist, so extremist, so unwilling to listen, how they are so sure they're right, just like she was, and worst of all, how they insist that everything they find and everything they think of is theirs, is new, is original, has no past and doesn't really need much of a future –

which is the amount of future she worries they will get.

Zoe worries about how it's probably true what Frost said in that poem she first heard when she was 13 – way *does* lead on to way, so we never get back again, even when going back might be, would be, looks like, a good idea.

THE OPTIMISTIC CHILD

Nawal el Sa'adawi

I don't know why, but I am optimistic by nature. The child inside me can often offer great hope for what the future holds in store for women, as we approach the twenty-first century. But sometimes this child disappears, especially when I consider my region, the 'Middle East'. It is clear from the very term itself that it is others who have named us in relation to their position in the world. If I was to describe Britain, for example, I could say it is in the 'Middle West', and the United States of America would be the 'Far West'. But do you think this will happen in the coming millennium?

I am a novelist, a writer who refuses to play the game. In Egypt, my country, you cannot carry the title of a 'Great Writer' unless you are friendly with those in power. Under Sadat I was not even considered a writer (let alone a great one) while others suddenly became Great Writers, and still carry the title today. This is not specific to Egypt or to my region. I have discovered that most of the writers who have won the Nobel prize for literature have good relations with those in power, nationally or internationally. I will never win the Nobel prize even if I live to the third or fourth millennium!

Everywhere I go in the 'Middle West' or 'Far West' I am asked about my identity – my nationality, gender, age, class, religion, culture, politics and sexuality. If my answers do not fit, they are not recorded. The international media, just like our national media, is controlled. It is not free, except when 'freedom' is interpreted as the 'freedom of the powerful to do whatever they like'.

To be a writer (not a great one) you have to know how words play games. The most famous word in the twentieth century (and probably in the next) is 'peace'. It looks wonderful on paper and at conferences and we are bombarded with the word every day by the media. Yet, almost every morning I also hear fresh news of bombing and bloodshed, of massacres, of people killed in my region. The more I live in this world the more I discover 'war' hidden beneath the word peace, injustices masquerading as justice, dictatorship disguised as democracy, and colonialism presented as protection or freedom. We have never known real peace and more and more people are killed every day: in Palestine, Iraq, Algeria, Sudan, Zaïre, Rwanda, Pakistan, Afghanistan...

A few days ago an innocent child was shot dead by Israeli soldiers, his mother and sisters abused and killed, their house demolished. I saw the photograph in the newspapers. The house was knocked down by bulldozers. Why? No reason except that they were Palestinians. When your nationality is not the 'right one', when your gender and class are against you, what do you do as we enter the twenty-first century?

On 1 July 1997 I participated in a demonstration in the streets of New York, in front of the tall building of the United Nations. Children organised the demonstration. Their aim was to stop all the economic embargoes in the world. In Iraq alone, 450 children die of hunger every day because of the embargo. After the demonstration we met top officials in the UN. It became evident in the course of the meeting that the UN has no power, and is dominated by the interests of the United States of America. We now call the UN 'The

United Nations of America' (UNA)! If you have nuclear military power and possess the veto in the UN security council you do not need to abide by international law or the UN charter. You can violate all laws and all UN resolutions and still be right, legal and respected.

'Power' is the *real* key word of the twentieth century and the next century and the next, so long as we are governed by the capitalist patriarchal system. Injustices based on race, gender, class, nationality, religion, etc., can all be justified in the name of God, the state, the free market, the husband or the father. Power can be used to turn laws, agreements, understandings on their heads. Double standards are the universal law.

From economic embargoes to inappropriate technologies, from resource depletion and environmental degradation to increasing women's veiling and circumcision – these are just some of the problems we suffer in our region. They are not seen by the West as the result of an unbalanced global and local ruling system, but as the result of underdevelopment, our lack of intelligence, our inability to rise to higher levels of morality and spirituality. Why? It is our black or brown colour, our religion or culture as Muslims or Arabs.

US aid to poor countries always comes with strings attached, with demands for religious, constitutional or cultural change a condition of aid. Anything can be used or abused to hide certain political or economic gains.

The free market sends us bad food, bad meat and nuclear waste. It is the freedom of the powerful to exploit and deceive. International and national laws require either explicitly or implicitly that a small country be obedient to a big country and thus make countries in my region vulnerable to military and economic sanctions. Just as in the family, religions legitimise the husband's disciplining of the wife, which then makes women vulnerable to physical abuse. The UN security council codes and vetoes help to reinforce the oppressive aspect of the international obedience law exactly as the family code helps to enforce the wife's obedience to her husband.

Major religions historically supported and justified slavery. Judaism, Christianity and Islam relied on the story of Noah in the holy books. Noah awakes drunk and naked, and curses his youngest son, Ham, because he saw the nakedness of his father. The father is like God: he does not see his own faults, instead he punishes the weaker, the youngest dark-skinned little boy, the scapegoat. Ever since then victims have been punished instead of the sinful masters. The curse of Noah on Canaan (the black child of Ham) justified the inferiority of the Canaanites, their subsequent destruction and the invasion of their land (the Promised Land).

Christianity has played an important role in the control of slaves and in the enforcement of slave codes in the New World. Christian spiritual doctrine, as well that of other world religions, has legitimised hierarchical orders on earth. All these religions preached to women and slaves that they were incapable of governing themselves and therefore were better off in slavery, and should accept their servile position as part of God's order.

Despite the progress accomplished during the twentieth century towards a new theological position mandating the abolition of slavery and the end of the oppression of women, most contemporary fundamentalist groups (governmental and non-governmental) continue to justify the oppression of women and poor working people, under the veil of morality, spirituality and family values.

In the USA and other Western Christian societies there has been a history of explicit and implicit laws which prohibit equality between men and women or between people of colour and white people. Almost all types of racial, sexual and class discrimination are based on the so-called divine plan, on the spiritual superpower in heaven, behind which the material superpower on earth operates.

Some Western circles maintain that women's oppression is linked to Islam alone. But this contention is only their way of reinforcing their own superiority, and in my region is part of the international political game. It provokes Muslims to defend their religion, and others to defend theirs.

The debate is now, as ever, a religious one. For great economic gain, the Christian USA funds numerous conflicts between supposedly 'superior' and 'inferior' cultures. In my region, for instance, the Arab–Israeli conflict is cultural and religious – between Muslims and Jews. Daily we have bombing, bloodshed, sanctions, thousands of people killed, and it is all part of the global and local political economic game.

My hope for the future is that the optimistic child within me will perhaps reawaken one day to a world where regional conflict and Western intervention are a thing of the past; where 'war' and 'power' will be outdated words; or where, at the very least, the word 'peace' will actually represent a realistic goal.

CROSSING THE LINE

Bulbul Sharma

Miss India smiles through her tears, adjusting the Miss World crown with her glittering fingernails, and Ranimala is sold by her father for 800 rupees. Both girls were born in the same state, and probably even saw each other fleetingly on some crowded street, but they live in totally different worlds and will continue to do so. They are sharply divided by Laxman Rekha – the mythological line women are forbidden to cross, in the *Ramayan*.

India crawls into the twenty-first century weighed down like a python by her 960 million people, caught between the wealth of a few and the poverty of the majority. In Bombay a bride is weighed in gold as bottles of champagne pop around her head, while on the pavement outside children scratch their festering wounds as they beg for one rupee coins. In the ancient temples of Varanasi idols are bathed in milk, butter and honey, while child widows fight for rice thrown away by the pilgrims. Everywhere we travel, in every city we live, the stark contrast glares at us as sharp as sunlight, but we have, over the years, learned to look away and erase these images from our minds with a quick turn of our heads.

'Look at our achievements,' we scream to the outside world if anyone dares to point a finger at us. We talk about our brilliant scientists, our modern city planners, our successful space programmes, and we feel good for a moment or two. But when we go out into the streets, the staring eyes of a beggar, who died last night on the pavement, stay with us.

As we approach the year 2000, the future is looking very different from our recent past. Vast amounts of money are being spent on official celebrations, endless seminars for and by the intelligentsia, and brand-new welfare plans by the government, yet the disparities widen at a steady pace and the scales tilt even more unevenly. Multinational companies come streaming in with dazzling electric colours and sounds. In remote villages children now hum the Coca-Cola jingle as they take their buffaloes to graze. In tattered clothes and skins grey with malnutrition, they laugh with joy as they see strange, magical toys that talk, dance and glow. They would like to get a closer look, but the only colour television set in their village is always surrounded by a huge crowd. They would like to touch a Barbie doll just once to see whether her golden hair is real. And these Nike shoes – 'Do they really make you fly?' they wonder.

Whereas in Delhi the rich heave a sigh of relief. 'I do not need to go abroad to get anything any more. TV sets, CD players, cars, deodorants, clothes – you name it – we get them here. It is great to be in India now with all this fantastic stuff available. McDonald's, KFC, Nike – everything and everyone is here,' says Nikhil, a young executive who lives with his eyes fixed firmly on the golden India of the twenty-first century. There are many like him who feel proud of India's new glossy look, an India where they can shut their eyes and imagine themselves to be in New York, London or Paris. The tinted windows of their air-conditioned Mercedes keep the sounds and smells of the other India safely away. The middle classes, too, are happy as they march ahead with more money in their pockets to spend on luxury goods they never had before. 'My father could never even afford a second-hand car, though he worked so hard, but I have managed to buy two cars and a flat in Delhi. My wife earns well too and we have saved enough to go for holidays each year. We will go to Vaishno Devi first to thank the Goddess for the new car she gave us.'

Our Gods and Goddesses, more than a thousand of them, hold on tight as we approach the twenty-first century. Millions of Indians, both rich and poor, go each year on a pilgrimage to Vaishno Devi to seek her blessings: to ask for a son, to thank her for favours she has bestowed, to show her a new car. The rich pilgrims can now buy time-share apartments here, while the poor travel by foot to this corner of India to touch Vaishno Devi's granite feet. But they never ask for favours like drinking water in their villages, protection from upper-caste violence, or food for their children.

As one small part of India reaches for the moon and strides ahead with pride; enjoying the benefits of a free, literate, open society; debating art, culture and politics; the lives of millions of other Indians hover around the poverty line, a situation that has remained unchanged for centuries. They do not know or care about the new millennium because their lives have been frozen in another age, where children are sacrificed to appease the Gods, upper-caste men kill those born below them in the caste pyramid, and women are paraded naked and raped as punishment just because they stole food for their starving children. This India lives and dies as it has done silently for the last millennium. We, the well fed, the educated, blame the government, the politicians, the corrupt foreign powers, while the women of the other India wait in the shadows, watching their children eat leaves to ward off the final pangs of hunger before death. Still they sing with joy when the first monsoon rain falls and thank the heavens for one bowl of rice.

India will survive anything, as it has done for

centuries. We have an extraordinary capacity to overcome both natural and man-made disasters and make ourselves whole again, however badly broken and wounded we are in our battle for survival. We sing, dance, eat, travel, marry, give birth, mourn our dead and pray to our hundred thousand Gods with a passion which is totally, and uniquely, Indian.

THE NEXT THOUSAND YEARS

Andrea Dworkin

If I could make a wish for the next millennium it would be for an end to genocide, mass murder, rape and prostitution. And I'd like to see flowers everywhere, especially near cement and concrete, walls and fences, bus stops and taxi stands, school playgrounds and corporate skyscrapers. Why not?

But what will happen is ugly: thuglike nuclear terrorism; the normalisation of sex trafficking in women and girls; the extermination of rebellious women, made easy because human cloning will finally put reproduction in the hands of men; Christian, Muslim and Jewish fundamentalism destroying rights-based law, especially for women; the global acceptance of female child brides and female child whores; mass destruction of females through sex-selected abortion and female infanticide; the arming of men with big guns, bombs, grenades, poisons, and chemical and biological weapons; a universal polemic in art and music that celebrates the rape and murder of women and girls; live sexual sadism against women and children as mass entertainment; executions broadcast as pay-per-view cable events; real murder, real rape, real assault eclipsing fiction – broadcast as news and entertainment; more contract killers and more serial killers, each with a subculture of romance and celebration.

US pop-culture imperialism will overtake all

traditional cultures, which will be respected only when they disadvantage women, for example, clitoral excision or segregation and captivity. As the rich get richer and the poor get poorer, middle-aged and older women will increasingly be homeless, on the streets; food, shelter and literacy won't be wasted on women. The women's literature from the last half of the twentieth century will be erased, gone, buried; no women's movement will be documented in history books. Feminists will be visible only in pornographic scenarios as stereotypically cartoonish uppity women, made happy and normal through rape – incestuous rape, anal rape, sadistic rape. (For those who like high culture, *The Taming of the Shrew* will last; it's got at least another thousand years.)

Think of Gettysburg or Normandy. There will be unmarked graveyards, mile after mile, women killed in an undeclared war. Anonymous women; pseudonymous women; unknown and silent women; tears; bones, shattered, blunted, splintered bones; crushed bones; bones in the fingers and pubic bones; acre after acre; bones.

We had a chance in the last decades of the twentieth century. We could have closed down the pornography industry; retaliated against child rapers and wife rapers; put johns in our own prisons; demanded reparations for every female body bought and sold; overthrown governments that protected sex trafficking; created secret governments that put women and children first; educated girls to read *and* fight; killed pimps; redistributed money and cars and clothes and shoes and food; murdered murderers and raped rapists.

We could have negotiated peace – the women, Palestinian and Israeli; the women, Northern Ireland and England; the women, Greeks and Turks; the women, the women, the women. We used to have a talent for making peace; or has it been fucked out of us? Can we remember – what he did; and him; and him? Can we remember – the girl coming up now, who she is and what she must have? Can we remember – what we almost did: near victory, which is the worst kind of failure? Can we remember – what we wanted? Can we remember – not to supplicate, not to beg? Can we remember to organise? to demonstrate? to resist? to rebel? to be treasonous against male authority? Can we remember how? Can we remember why?

Over two thousand years of human history will have passed; and still women and girls will be sold for sex, now in an international market. In Eastern Europe the 'free market' means the prostituting of women. In India the 'free market' means the aborting of female fetuses. In the US the 'free market' joined to 'free speech' means the unrestricted pimping of women in pornography and pandemic sexual violence against women and girls. How much more 'free' can we stand? We've betrayed the future by defending the present, the status quo, by clinging to what does not move, by holding on, tenacious, stubborn, stupid, to the static paradigm of him over her. We were greedy – for pleasure or profit or sex or love or attention or approval; we were cowards – we gave in; we were sentimental – we wanted to bring him-over-her with us, drag him-over-her forward, a nicer him, a more equal her. My prayer for the women of the next millennium: have hard hearts; and learn how to kill.

WOMAN TO WOMAN

Emma Mashinini and Mphoentle Mageza

Emma Mashinini

At long last women are involved in shaping government, business and education in South Africa. The sweeping aside of the Apartheid state was one of the great achievements of the last years of the twentieth century, and women – especially black women – played a key role in this.

Land has always been a precious commodity and close to the hearts of South Africans. During the Apartheid era 87 per cent was owned by whites and 13 per cent by Africans. The changes here are great, and as a Land Commissioner, I find settling the claims for restoration of land to the original owners one of the high points of our new democracy – particularly as women are the greatest users of land, something that is confirmed again and again as I travel my country in the course of my work.

The new generation of women has to apply themselves, and work and study hard to challenge and contribute to the laws that govern the country. I enjoy witnessing implementors: parliament includes a young generation of women who have demonstrated that they can do it. I boast about being a good role model and young women have acknowledged this and drawn strength from it. One such woman is Mphoentle Mageza – my granddaughter – who I have asked to join me in this article.

*

Mphoentle Mageza

My own life as a woman – as my mother's daughter, my grandmother's granddaughter, as my sister's sister and my aunt's niece – has defined me in immeasurable ways. Few things have defined me more. My world-view has, for better or worse, been shaped by these women's lives, their joy and their pain.

There are so many things I could write about these women so I have decided that I will write about what intrigues me the most – their strength, resilience and instinct for survival.

The day I came 'of age', was when I first was able to identify my own strength as a woman. On a fateful day in April 1988, my father, Aubrey Ntsikiwane Mageza, was violently killed by a mob in Soweto, Johannesburg. In some ways, he was a casualty of the times; times when unfounded rumours led to tragedy, when distrust hung like a shadow over our lives. Times when innocent people were caught in the crossfire, in the cauldron that was South African politics.

A rumour had been making the rounds in Soweto, that ambulance and hearse drivers were kidnapping children in the townships. These were the types of lies the Apartheid government used to disseminate in the townships to destabilise the community. They wanted us to hate and kill each other. My family ran a funeral business and the tragedy had occurred when my father tried to save an employee who had been driving one of our hearses from the hands of an angry, wild mob. Both died violently at the hands of the irrational crowd. The women of my family were not there when it happened, but within one hour our lives had changed completely, for ever.

I was about 14 years old then and today, at age 24, I think back to that time...

*

My mother, my sister and I were sitting in our home waiting for news of my father who we understood had gone to help his colleague. We were very worried, but I believed he would be back soon – my father was my invincible hero after all. Then ten or more women from the neighbourhood came to our front gate covered in blankets and cloths, a sign of respect and humility. This was something I was unaccustomed to as I had spent most of my childhood in Germany, but I knew something was wrong. Everything was happening so quickly – my maternal grandmother, Emma, arrived. (My sister and I called her 'Gògo', which means grandmother.) Trying to look composed she packed us into her car and drove us to her place. It later turned out that some women from the neighbourhood had called her about my father's death, and asked her to break the news.

When I think back to that day, what always stands out in my mind are those women. In their support and courage, they had come out immediately in their numbers. While we were waiting to hear some definite news, we were very composed. Nothing serious could be the matter...right? In the meantime, I had casually called my aunts, and they came with their husbands and we waited. To be honest, due to anxiety and shock I do not remember much of what happened after I heard about my father's death, but the next day my mother was sitting in our parents' bedroom on a mattress, covered in blankets and wearing headgear. It is part of our tradition and mourning ritual to strip the bed, and the widow sits on the mattress all day and all night to allow other people to visit her and grieve with her through song and prayer. Throughout the period preceding the funeral there are women who keep her company and act as counsellors; giving her advice and lending her enormous support. Early in the mornings they also take the widow on short walks and perform stretch movements before any guests arrive, understanding the need for exercise and contact with nature. All day women are coming in and out of the house, cooking, baking, praying, singing and cleaning.

Later, I found out that my aunt in the USA (who I affectionately call 'Mamane', which means 'small/younger mother'), had phoned the day after the tragedy because she had had a strange feeling that something awful had happened. Several days later she arrived in Johannesburg and took on the role of mother to me and my sister. She dressed us, cooked for us and made sure we got to school every day.

As big sister I felt I should be very strong and helpful, but I was overwhelmed to say the least. I could not quite comprehend what was happening, I was distracted and distraught.

Throughout the week leading up to the funeral, we went to school. My mother insisted that we carry on with our lives, and every day she tried to smile for us when we proudly showed her our test marks and schoolwork. We thought that sharing our achievements with her was the least we could do, although it was difficult for us as we struggled with our own grief.

A few days before the funeral, as my Gogo and Leah Tutu picked us up from school, my sister privately asked Leah if she would stand in for her at the funeral, if my sister was asked to make a speech. For a moment there, a young child showed maturity and concern beyond her age. My sister was about ten years old at the time, and she shared her concerns and made a request not merely as a child, but as a human being, a woman to another woman.

The funeral came and went and then came the hard part, getting back to 'normal' life. We lived for a short while with my paternal grandmother, a woman who needed every ounce of her strength to deal with the pain of being a mother who had outlived her son. But continued threats from certain people, who believed my father had done something wrong, meant eventually we had to move on.

My mother single-handedly built her children a new home, the most beautiful in the area, in a new settlement born out of the death of the Apartheid state and its policy of 'separate development'. In the past both my mother and grandmother had refused to settle in the 'white' areas, because they would have had to ask their neighbours for permission to move in – one of the many almost incredible strictures of the Apartheid laws!

So there we were in our new home, and day in and day out we kept on going. Day in and day out my mother kept on smiling for us. Today, ten years and five months later, I am 24 years old and completing a Master's degree in the United States, and I have also embarked on an exciting career as a journalist. My sister, who is as sweet as ever, is studying International Relations at the University of Cape Town. The more successful we become the more sensitive and aware I become of my mother's sacrifices to send us to the best schools, continue to allow us to travel the world, put food on the table every single day and dress us well. Single-handedly she gave us the best of the best and never said 'No, I can't'. She instilled a work ethic in us few can match and she taught us to say 'Please. Thank you. Sorry. Can I help you. I love you.' Single-handedly.

Then there is that other woman in my life, my grandmother, Emma 'Tiny' Mashinini. I say her name with pride and admiration. The first memory I have of her is when she visited us in Germany, some time in the

1980s. I remember being extremely interested in this short, exquisitely dressed and highly talkative woman. I did not know at the time that she had earned her success and respect the hard way. For a black woman in her senior years to have done well in South Africa during Apartheid you had to be an overachiever. As I grew older, I learnt that she had not completed high school and had grown up, like most black South Africans, in poverty. Through hard work and phenomenal courage, she had founded a powerful trade union, making history more than once. I remember being told that she had been in prison because of her political activities, but I did not really understand this at the time. Now I do.

But what I appreciate most about her life and what has affected me most positively is that she walked out on two abusive marriages. For a black woman to terminate a marriage, even under the most extreme circumstances, has been taboo in our community. She took control of her life when nobody, least of all her partners, expected her to, and she decided that her life, integrity and sanity came first. Unknowingly, she set a high standard for me to follow. I now know that I will never tolerate an abusive relationship. Ever. What greater gift exists to be given than the gift of integrity? Woman to woman, through example.

The differences and similarities between the older and younger generations in South Africa interest me deeply. Yesterday the struggle was a political one and today the struggle is of an economic nature. Can my generation of women ever hope to fill the shoes of our mothers and grandmothers?

All these brave women struggled for and victoriously achieved, has to be appreciated and carried further. I feel a great sense of responsibility and humility when I speak to Brigalia Barn, Joyce

Seroke, Pusetso Mbalane, Leah Tutu, Frene Ginwala and, of course, my grandmother, and what I want to know is: 'What do you want me to do? How can I fill your shoes? Give me a mission!'

Instinctively, I know what my mission is and it is petrifyingly simple – to be the best I can possibly be and stay true to myself. Being a black woman in South Africa is a blessing at the moment as today's woman is free – free to pursue her dreams without fear. By giving the previously disadvantaged priority, black women have been placed right at the top of the list. It is expected that with hard work, a positive attitude and a black skin, one should be successful. Of course, there is a lot of pressure to do well and an equal amount of fear of being perceived as a failure.

We are all women of the twenty-first century. We will reap the benefits of a democratic country. Ironically, along with this freedom comes a lot of uncertainty and an intense competitiveness. The pie looks a lot smaller than it actually is and for the new millennium we need to acquire an 'abundance' mentality: that there is enough for everyone and that through sharing we can multiply our wealth – an important lesson that the older generation is acutely aware of. The younger generation has been thrown into an exciting and unpredictable world, almost completely unprepared, and this is where insecurity, mutual envy and suspicion can originate.

How does one run a government when one was denied access to government for generations? How does one excel in a corporate environment when decent education and training was strategically kept from one? 'Strength lies in numbers' is the old adage. How do a few fortunate women help those many less fortunate? It is difficult and sometimes disheartening, and the only sure way of gaining direction and support is by looking to the older generation of women for wisdom and inspiration.

My mother and grandmother have instilled in me the belief that even under the most difficult situations, with faith, integrity, respect and hard work anything can be achieved, but we need to find our own formula. They discovered a winning formula on their own and we have to develop an even stronger strategy in the same way. The starting point is our instinct, an age-old gift that women have long appreciated and used.

We will feel our way through things and one day, we will be pillars of strength to our younger sisters, children and grandchildren. Their dreams will be our dreams.

DAWNINGS

Zelda Curtis

One Monday is much the same as any other, but as this one dawns, just ten years into the new century, I enjoy a few more restful moments in bed, eyes closed, listening to the clinking of cups on saucers as Nick makes the tea. I look forward to these morning cuppas, sitting up in bed talking of things past and looking forward with high hopes to the future. I was always an optimist, and although over the years this has been tempered with a touch of reality, I remain hopeful for this twenty-first century when I see the confidence of the younger women around me. They walk tall. It was their mothers who started to challenge the male-oriented world. They are now reaping the benefits.

Share with me a glance back at my generation's experience of the last half of the twentieth century and the dawning of the new millennium. I was one of the generation of women that broke free from home and family restrictions when we joined the armed forces during the Second World War. Our horizons widened, our expectations were high, but they were soon dashed at the end of the war, when we were pushed back into the home to service the returning war heroes. Frustration set in and the life-changing books of Betty Friedan and Marilyn French had not yet been published...

Marriages broke up. After six years of war, the virgin brides the men had left behind had become independent and worldly-wise; and the fresh-faced youths the women remembered had come back vastly changed. Their very different experiences of the war years had driven a wedge between them. Several of my friends got divorced. What saved my own marriage was our newly shared interest in political activity, after the landslide victory of Attlee's Labour government. Then, with the nuclear build-up and the Cold War, we joined the peace movement and took part in huge torchlight marches to save the Rosenbergs from the electric chair. And later, our daughters joined us on CND marches, anti-Vietnam demonstrations and anti-Apartheid vigils.

Almost overnight it seemed we saw our daughters change before our very eyes into flower-power hippies and counter-cultural activists. The music of the Doors and Fairport Convention filled the house; their boyfriends wore their hair long and lazed about my front room smoking marijuana and listening to John Peel. The house was always abuzz with argument.

Life seemed very tame when they upped and left home, one to University, the other to Art College; one becoming a student revolutionary, the other a squatter.

My mind was churning with all the new ideas floating around. Then the Women's Liberation Movement took centre stage, the personal became political, and everything changed for me and so many other women of my age. Our horizons expanded as we began to absorb the new ideas, learn the new woman-friendly language, and look at the world through women's eyes – the eyes of the talented new women writers, psychiatrists and philosophers. My world became women-centred. Those were heady days; everything seemed to change so quickly. The contraceptive pill and the Abortion Act had given women greater control over their own bodies as well as greater sexual freedom. Women's Centres sprang up everywhere. Women entered the manual trades, started to climb the ladders of success in business and professions. Women's theatre flourished, women's bands filled the local venues, and lesbians marched with pride through the streets of London. And I was in the thick of it all. It was then, in my sixties, that I started an Older Women's Group, and we made a film for the BBC TV *Open Door* programme. I was co-opted on to the Women's Committee of the GLC and later on Islington's Women's Committee, through which we fought for equal opportunities for women to become firefighters.

Local authorities were the trailblazers of equal opportunities policies, and arguments raged fiercely in the voluntary sector. In time they were firmly established on paper, but not always in practice. And still ageism persisted. Older women remained invisible and unheard, even among their feminist sisters. Then the '30-somethings' began to hit their heads on the glass ceilings of their professions. Male violence still persisted and the eating disorders of the younger generation of women became a major worry. Even those men dubbed 'new men' were found not to be doing their equal share of work in the home or of childcare, while the media declared feminism to be over. Feminists puzzled as to how to overcome this backlash – but young women still seemed confident of their equal place in the sun and strode ahead of the boys in the educational stakes.

Finishing my Millennium-Monday tea, with pale shafts of wintry light flickering across the bed, I ponder on the whys and wherefores and turn my thoughts to the future. Who could have foreseen the great medical advances of the end of the twentieth century that enabled me to move into the twenty-first century in good health and enjoy my eighty-fifth year free of the Parkinson's Disease that had so limited my life for eighteen years? It is very heartening to have lived to see some of my hopes fulfilled.

The end of the twentieth century was a time of great hardship for young women struggling to support their children in the face of a hostile society. But in getting together to help themselves, they have wrought tremendous changes in society – changes that are of the 'stuff that dreams are made of'! Let me paint you a word picture of what life is like now.

My small but cosy flat is in a block of twelve, collectively owned and managed, with a large communal area on the ground floor alongside the computer room, which is open to all users. We are part of a small estate with just five other similar blocks, each having a different usage for the ground floor – one has a swimming pool, another a gym. There's an art studio in one and a music workshop in another, and the last houses a large meeting room. In the middle of the estate there is a small clinic with a visiting doctor and chiropodist, and a sizeable space is left for the nursery and crèche. At one end of the estate there is a plot of land for growing fruit and vegetables, which boosts the supply of foodstuffs on sale at our Food Co-Op. Nick and I run the Co-Op, because we are normally up very early and don't have to get any children off to school, so we can go to the market early enough to get the best bargains. We also hold a few study classes in the meeting room, as well as participating in the University of the Third Age. There really is something for everyone, and everyone plays their part.

Remembering the old days of large-scale unemployment and all the ills that sprang from that, I am happy to say that the workforce is organised in a far better way now. No one has to work more than a three-day shift for a wage sufficient for their needs, and they are paid equally, regardless of age or sex.

Many partners share jobs as well as the work in the home. This is the Leisure Age.

The estate is car-free and the local shopping area is pedestrianised. Public transport is low-priced and accessible and the nearby canal is well used to get to the City.

So, where's the catch? you ask. No catch, although there are still some people who can't get out of old habits and old ideas. They grumble and grouch, and stand in council elections, trying to play their power games still. But they get few votes. Power bullies get short shrift in the meetings of the collective and policy-making assemblies.

However, alongside all of this, relationships are still problematic, despite the better living conditions. But no one is enclosed within four walls as previous generations were, and all of us on the estate give support to each other in times of difficulty. We don't encroach but are there if needed. Patience and openness in talking things through together are what's needed to get relationships working properly. I now recognise that it is more difficult to sort out personal relations than social ones. Emotions toss us backward and forward and men still have difficulty dealing with this side of themselves. Women, as ever, are more likely to be able to openly explore and discuss their feelings. It's going to take a long time yet to change these human traits. The push me/pull me problem remains stubborn.

Why on earth did we take so long to come to our senses and organise our society more equitably?

Don't answer that. I know, really, and I am pleased beyond measure to be able to say that it was women organising for change that brought it about.

In that long-ago time of the 1970s and '80s I played a part in a movement for co-operative housing and alternative working arrangements established in the

North East. Everyone was so enthusiastic and hard-working. We seemed to be succeeding for a short while, but the times were not right, or perhaps we weren't the right ones to be tackling this task. It failed. People were so money- and power-oriented then.

But enough of looking back. I have learned from those experiences and I am proud to be a part of the present 'caring and sharing' society. Now I am going out to revel in my pollution-free zone as I stroll down to the canal path to join the women and men fishing down there. There's always a good discussion to be had with someone down by the canal. That's what I like, having a good talk with someone on how to change the world – oh dear, I forgot, it has already been changed, and more than once in my lifetime!

I'll stay in bed a little longer.

SUSTAINABILITY: THE BIG PICTURE

Rosalie Bertell

On the eve of the year 2000, we find ourselves in a rapidly growing 'global community', being threatened with the 'Asian (Financial) Flu', struggling under personal and governmental debt, and facing a somewhat uncertain future. Although we have been told that the 'Cold War' is over, there is no real peace or peace dividend, and preparations for Star Wars proceed unabated. Although the global crisis is seen by those in power to be financial, it is most likely both a structural crisis of major proportions and a resource crisis due to so many years of externalising the true cost of our life styles to the family and the environment. We are, and have been for a number of years, using up the Earth's vast resources at a rate which exceeds its ability to replenish itself. We are also rapidly transferring wealth from the poor to the rich within nations, and from the poor countries to the rich countries globally.

As nations compete both for economic and military superiority, they significantly usurp Earth's resources, depriving the poor and the civilian economy of their birthright. If these resources are used in war, then more of the fragile Earth system is destroyed. Women and children usually bear the brunt of such destruction! Furthermore, in the name of trade, harmful products are being produced and sold, like pesticides and pseudo-oestrogens, which further poison the Earth and reduce its fertility.

Again, women and children are the most vulnerable!

The United Nations is perhaps our single hope for making this transition into a global community orderly and not chaotic! It was deliberately created as a 'weak' organisation, to be dominated by the Great Powers. However, in its direct appeal to the people of the planet, the UN has shown itself to be a strong force for air, water, land, human rights and the progress of people. For this reason, I propose the reform and strengthening of the UN as one of the most urgent needs of the twenty-first century. With some structural reform and the backing of the people, the UN can make significant progress toward forming liveable bioregional communities on a peaceful intact Earth.

Over a quarter century after the first United Nations Conference on the Environment, held in 1972, none of the major problems have seen any improvement! The ozone layer is disappearing at a faster rate than was predicted. All people of the Earth are experiencing weather extremes and climate change. Greenhouse gases continue to be spewed out. The nuclear power industry is poised for a major push to implement its technology in the developing countries – the Chernobyl disaster has been officially written off and the continued plight of the Chernobyl victims is being ignored for the sake of rescuing a failed industry and preparing the world to tolerate more radiation pollution of their air, water, land and food after the next nuclear disaster!

As decision makers encourage industry to triumphantly return to the past (failed) unlimited growth scenario, as if Earth had infinite resources, and the UN goal of sustainability falls further and further behind in the public mind, scientists are beginning to talk about saving life on the planet until the next century in the face of daily severe losses of species. There used to be a much longer time line! However, in the face of this gloomy future I am daring to hope for a spectacular human breakthrough to a more rational living pattern and a deeper understanding of the gift of life.

Over the last 50 years, the various agencies of the United Nations have evolved rather miraculously into more or less effective agents for global change. This is a remarkable accomplishment made difficult by the multinational/multilingual nature of its staff and the escalating nature of its mandate. The world's expectations of it are awesome, and it has endured great financial insecurity. Because the United Nations lacked physical coercive power from the beginning, not having a monopoly on lethal weapons and forces as have nation states, it has developed the more traditional feminine qualities of consensus building and moral persuasion. Recently, through a quick succession of international conferences, the United Nations has been building a strong global consensus for more responsible use of the environment – sustainable development, well thought-out human settlements, respect for human rights, and addressing of population concerns and the rights of women and children. While this consensus has not yet been translated into action, I believe that its vitality will prevail over the other very strong movements within the United Nations to orient the world body to serve the needs of global trade in an aggressive market economy.

As the Western world moves from military competition to exerting firm control over world trade policies, it has been attempting to use the United Nations to consolidate its control over intellectual property, patenting of nature and natural processes, and promoting constant national growth scenarios together with production of unlimited amounts of often superfluous consumer products. Individual governments have played on addictions to gambling and lotteries as a source of money to fund social programmes, while these methods are really ways of exploiting the poor and lowering taxes for the well off. The public's fear of crimes, and criminals addicted to alcohol and drugs, has become an excuse for greater police force and suppression of legitimate dissent.

One is reminded of the techniques used by Adolph Hitler in forming ghettos. He declared that it was necessary to isolate the Jewish people because they had contagious diseases. He prescribed ghettos as a public health policy. Then he controlled the jobs available in the ghettos and the health care available, but left the ghettos free to govern themselves. As jobs were poorly paid, food expensive, living conditions more crowded, and outward mobility prohibited, the problems of contagious diseases, of course, escalated. This reinforced the false logic, and exerted pressure on ghetto leaders who were taking the blame for conditions. However, the situation was unsustainable, and Hitler soon reverted to outright murder, without a great public outcry.

With today's globalisation of money and trade, goes ghettoisation of nations, labour exploitation, restriction of worker mobility, control of jobs and health care, and monetary structural adjustment which denies social assistance to the most needy. This is again an unsustainable situation. The harsh structural adjustment policies of the International Monetary Fund, meant to help the world's poorest countries to achieve honourable and dependable status among the global decision makers, have only further crushed the poor, fuelled riots and toppled governments.

It seems to me that the global trade and economic war we are experiencing offers an unsustainable scenario similar to that of Hitler's. It imposes the 'logic' of structural adjustment within struggling nations with developing economies, which in turn brings to the people poverty, sickness and crime, with no escape. The 'cure' creates the problem, and the policy will continue to create very unstable situations in the world. Such instability, with the poor growing poorer and the rich growing richer, cannot be 'managed' with brute force and suppression for long. When it breaks down, will it tend toward genocide again, or will there be an alternative answer which will rally human support from all parts of the world? There are clear signs that force will be tried, as in Bosnia and other so-called ethnic wars.

I see this problem made worse by the continued development of rocket technology, and efforts to control space. I see it in the continued development of high tech weapons: robots, space shields, and laser beams and the attempts by the US military to continue the work of the so-called 'Star Wars' programme. All of these projects demand use of scarce resources and finances, which are needed for life. What I believe is at stake, although the time line is not well known at present, is the way we will handle the unsustainable global scenario when the people of the world awaken and realise their plight. Obviously, those who propose the economic policies are the same ones who are preparing for the next war.

I believe that the war will be against the people who wish to share in the bountifulness of the Earth! There will likely be 'resource wars' between those who have access to the scarce supplies of water and food, and those who do not have such access. This means the aggressors are well aware that their economic and military policy recommendations are unsustainable! I do not see that a viable alternative consensus was available to those Germans who disagreed with Nazi policy in the 1930s and 1940s, but today we have real alternatives, and some encouraging signs of hope.

Greed, violence and short term goals will mean a 'good life' for a few people for a short time, but the ultimate destruction of the global environment and society as we know it. Ecological collapse is much more devastating than financial collapse. The alternative is widespread behavioural changes, and the adoption on a grand scale of attitudes, values and behaviours which lead to sustainable development. It has been slow in coming, but when one believes that life is stronger than death, one can stand against the tide and keep waiting and working for this change.

A vision of a sustainable development would need to include a healthy social, economic and natural environment. Poverty and unemployment are unsustainable 'pollution' of the social and economic environment. They have no place in the evolution of a healthy world order, one in which people can enjoy normal development of their potential and have healthy children. One of the means at the disposal of the United Nations to rectify the balance between social/environmental needs and those perceived needs of the economic and military communities, which tend to distort holistic development, is to strengthen the agencies which speak directly to the social and environmental needs. A second important option for the UN is to develop an International Environment Agency to see to the development of health based regulations and environmental protection laws which cannot be manipulated for trade advantages, and a specialised Court of the Environment to enforce these laws. The money for these new agencies could be obtained through closing down the branch of the International Atomic Energy Agency (IAEA) which has been mandated to promote nuclear energy. This task is certainly not needed in today's world! The so-called Tobin Tax, a tax on international financial transactions, could also provide funding for sustainable development programmes of the UN.

On 5 March 1997, the heads of the United Nations Environment Programme (UNEP) and the United Nations Children's Fund (UNICEF) signed a Memorandum of Understanding aimed at co-operation between these two programmes in areas fundamental to the attainment of sustainable development. Incidentally, both agency heads were women, Elizabeth Dowdeswell and Carol Bellamy. They have agreed to mutually supportive efforts, using the best available scientific and environmental information that bears on children and child health, to implement programmes to ensure the well being of children. Obviously, if we can maintain a good environment for children, the adults will also be able to reach their potential. Currently more than 12 million children die annually from preventable diseases. Pressures against children's survival come from poverty, the International Monetary Fund policy of structural adjustment, unfair trade practices, unemployment and underemployment of their parents, environmental degradation such as desertification, war and other counterproductive human 'behaviours'.

Whether or not this coalition of agencies will be strong enough to counteract the more aggressive policies of the World Trade Organisation will be seen in the future. However, UNEP, in particular, has been carefully building its credibility and reliability, especially among environmental and health professionals, and among the general population in economically developing countries. They have broad human support, even though they usually lack political and economic support.

The United Nations International Environment Agency and the International Court of the Environment were both proposed in Agenda 21 of the United Nations Conference on Environment and Development (UNCED) (also called the Earth Summit) in 1992, and they were approved by the participating nations. Judge Amedeo Postiglione of the Supreme Court of Italy has, with the backing of his country, been developing plans for the structure and functions of these two new UN Agencies. He needs more international support for this endeavour, which is important for maintaining the balance of power with the World Trade Organisation within the United Nations. Environmental protection is often called a trade barrier, and a level playing field is often the lowest and worst common denominator for workers rights and human health concerns!

And at a grass roots level, there is a tremendous movement for change. On 14 March 1997, the Environment Liaison Centre International in Kenya released its Tilonia Declaration, calling for a people-centred ecologically sustainable development model. This triennial meeting, held in Tilonia, Rajasthan, India, denounced trade and development practices that wipe out local culture, sustainable local practices and identities. This conference, in a remote village of the so-called Third World, has formally stated that: 'No sustainable solution to improve, preserve, protect and conserve the environment is possible without the direct involvement of communities in the planning and implementation process. Space must be created for the oppressed communities to participate in decision making.' People will no longer be sidelined and used to produce the wealth of others. Even the focus on biodiversity has aroused the passion for cultural diversity and healthy pride in one's heritage. Unlike the ghetto experience, local leaders are no longer being totally blamed for all local problems. People have begun to see the sources of pressure locally as connected with global economic and military plans, and the relentless destruction of the planet's resources.

This desire for grass roots participation in planning is an exact antithesis to the planning scheme behind the World Trade Organisation which has never sought grass roots input! In fact, the WTO would see trade as the highest 'good', taking precedence over social needs and civil liberties. It would shun democratic policies which it would see as biased toward human social needs over free markets (in spite of the fact that financial markets are anything but free).

Women have often been considered historically as the indicators of social rest or unrest. They often act as social change agents, having generated and organised most social institutions including schools, hospitals and social service agencies. Women have played a leading role in the United Nations social agencies including, as previously noted, Elizabeth Dowdeswell at UNEP, Carol Bellamy at UNICEF and Barbara Ward who was influential in putting the environment on the global agenda. The World Women's Conference in Beijing in 1995 was incredibly well attended and, for the first time in history, the Non-Governmental Organisations' Parallel Conference was better attended than the Governmental Conference. Women declared their firm conviction that Earth was to be lived in and nurtured, and survival of life was more urgent than the market economy.

The partners for a coalition of UN Agencies, People's Movements, Non-Governmental Organisations and Women's Movements are now in place. I would rate them as still politically weak in the face of money, nation-state military and economic power, but they are becoming a real moral force not easily ignored. If this were our only basis for hope, I would not be so optimistic about the future as I am. However, there is more to the story. A new seed has been cast in the human community, and if it takes root and grows it will, I think, be strong enough to assure that sanity will carry the balance of power. That 'wild card' may well be the Earth Charter, which set sail into the human global forum from the Rio + 5 Conference, organised by the Costa Rica-based Earth Council in March 1997.

When the United Nations was first launched in 1945, there was a poetic vision born with it to nourish its more practical structural components. This vision was embodied in the Human Rights Covenants. It is notable that these rights were not called 'democratic', but 'human'. Eleanor Roosevelt was the guiding hand which launched this document in the post war world. These Rights applied to every person born into this world and not just to those who were born in nations that had a democratic form of government. The Covenants set a limit on governmental power, no matter what its origin, structure or history. Governmental power was clearly declared to be limited by human rights.

This vision has given rise to many organisations, such as Amnesty International and the International Human Rights Lawyers, and the grass roots people of the world have found it a powerful friend. It has given pause to those who would abuse power, and even where it failed to moderate aberrant behaviour, it took away all pretence to social approval. Humans can change their behaviour, and withhold social approval of unacceptable behaviour, even when that behaviour was not questioned in the past. The great human victories in this regard have been over cannibalism, slavery, torture, oppression of women, exploitation of children and destruction of worker health. The struggle goes on to outlaw capital punishment, genocide and rape as weapons of war, and violence as a way to settle differences.

This tactic of sowing seeds of hope and vision, the Human Rights Covenants, along with structural creations, has helped all of the UN agencies and given them enormous credibility with all people. Even in the most restrictive times of the former Soviet rule, United Nations Programmes could be implemented. Developing nations hold the United Nations as their friend and mentor, and as a sign of hope in a hostile world.

In our day, we again have a new vision document with which we can grow over the next decades. If supported, this new vision statement will not only broaden the concept of good global citizenship, and articulate the values and behaviours acceptable in a developing global community, but it should effectively mould society's expectations. It can also be expected to spawn Non-Governmental Organisations which will take to heart this vision and give it life. The proposed opening statement of the Earth Charter is itself a breakthrough: 'Earth is our home and home to all living beings. Earth itself is alive.' This planet is not either a junkyard or a battlefield! For those women who struggle against discrimination and unjust social systems in order to bring up healthy children, the Earth Charter says: 'Establish justice, and defend without discrimination the right of all people to life, liberty, and security of person within an environment adequate for human health and spiritual well being. People have a right to potable water, clean air, uncontaminated soil, and food security.' There is, further, a call to live peacefully: 'Practice non-violence, recognising that peace is the wholeness created by harmonious and balanced relationships with oneself, other persons, other life forms and Earth.'

Some declarations from the Earth Charter particularly mention or further women's rights: 'Affirm that gender equality is a prerequisite for sustainable development. Secure the right to sexual and reproductive health, with special concern for women and girls...Ensure that people throughout their lives have opportunities to acquire the knowledge, values, and practical skills needed to build sustainable communities.'

Hopefully, the Earth Charter will also serve, as did the Human Rights Covenants, to reorient nationalism toward globalism in a world enriched with a countless variety of global villages, each with a distinctive culture and place in the tapestry being created. In turn, this will fulfil the human desire to nurture helpful differences in life style, and encourage the formation of bioregional coalitions for handling common problems. It should serve to reduce local government to maintaining viable local infrastructure and civil order. The reduction of competition should lead to resolving differences by legal means other than a law of the jungle type military violence, thus at the same time reducing the need for nation states. This would be expected to give rise to bioregional organisations where common energy, life style and transportation problems can find solutions. Political organisations will become relatively less important, and there will be no need to raise standing armies. Capable police and emergency response teams will be all that are needed to maintain peace among these global villages.

My hope for the future of the United Nations rests in structural reform, especially in the strengthening of the social and environmental agencies, in the development of international law, and in the power of the seed sown through the promulgation of the Earth Charter. The draft Charter was circulated widely during 1998, and is to be finalised soon. It is hoped that this Charter will then be formally accepted by the UN Committee on Sustainable Development, and sent on to the General Assembly for approval. It then becomes a Treaty, a new Covenant governing human relationships with the Earth and with all of the living creatures with whom we share this profound gift of life. As such, a new and fruitful era of human life on Earth may just be able to break through our misguided pursuit of money and power, which has undermined the survival of our planet. With a new vision, led by women's wisdom, we may be able to embrace life itself in a stunning realisation of our dignity and oneness with the universe. The twenty-first century may then be hailed as one which embodied for the first time an integration of knowledge with wisdom, and power with compassion.

NEWS FROM THE 21ST CENTURY

Vanessa Baird

Puerto Maldonado, Peru

'Would you like to come through now?'

The foreign correspondent uncrosses his long legs and follows a tiny woman, his eyes fixed on the plait of black hair dangling down her back.

Perhaps she is the presidential candidate's secretary? She doesn't look much like a secretary though, he reflects. More like a woman who sells mangoes in the market.

The timing for this interview is absolutely perfect. Opinion polls published this morning have shown a sudden, quite unpredicted swing in favour of the virtually 'unknown' contestant, who appears to have come out of nowhere. This candidate is unusual on a number of counts. First, she is female. Second she is neither white nor *mestizo* but a member of the indigenous Machiguenga group from the Amazon rainforest. Third she appears to have gained massive support with only a fraction of the media exposure of her opponents.

Her politics are hardly conventional. She is not offering tax cuts or other carrots. Rather she is standing on a ticket of 'respect' – respect for all other humans, respect for other species and respect for the environment.

The woman with the plait takes him into a spartan room containing a desk and three chairs. He takes a chair that is offered and waits for the presidential candidate to come in. The woman pulls up another chair next to him and waits. Perhaps she will sit in on the interview? He takes the opportunity to scribble a few more notes to himself, then looks at his watch.

'Would you like to start?' the woman says.

'Well yes, actually, do you think she will be long?'

'Not at all,' she replies. 'She is with you right now.'

Bangkok, Thailand

Kaew switches on the radio:

'As the protest goes into its fourth day the city is at a standstill. No cars or buses are able to...

Good, Kaew thinks. It means she and her seven-year-old daughter Sanyan can leave their masks behind.

They step out on to the street of the quiet capital. Never in all her years has Kaew known the city this way.

Her daughter suddenly stops in her tracks: 'What's that?'

Kaew strains to hear: 'A bird, sweetheart. It's a bird.'

A few electric buses – for the old or disabled – have been let through the blockade. People with small children have taken to strapping them on their backs, as their great grandparents used to do in the old days. Street artists and musicians give impromptu performances. Other city-dwellers simply take their pleasure by ambling down the middle of the usually traffic-choked avenues.

As they walk mother and daughter hear snatches of conversation. 'Do you know, I timed myself walking to work and it took less time than...'

The mood is upbeat at the infants' school. This is where it all started, when a group of mothers decided they had had enough of fossil-fuel pollution damaging their children's health.

The movement touched a nerve. Green guerrillas

went around immobilising parked cars. Armies of cyclists staged a take-over of the city centre streets, resurrecting a direct action tactic popular at the end of the last century. Other people sat down in their hundreds to blockade the main arteries into the city. Only emergency vehicles were allowed through.

As Kaew makes her way from the school to her office she passes a group of people gathered in front of a large TV screen, watching the news:

'...the movement seems to have gained the support of the majority of the capital's population. Copycat protests are now taking place in other cities around the world. Mexico City, Lagos, Athens and London...'

London, England

A series of embarrassing results is threatening the future of the controversial 'designer baby' programme, now in its fifth year. The programme was expected to enable ordinary couples to choose a range of physical characteristics for their offspring by the year 2010.

But the latest results have thrown scientists into confusion. Leading geneticist Dr Seema Jones admitted: 'The results are quite the opposite of what we expected. They suggest that genetically "designed" babies are actually far *less* likely to exhibit the traits chosen by their parents than if they had been developed without any genetic intervention at all. Some rogue traits have also entered the picture, while others have mutated in such a way as to produce caricatures of the desired traits.'

Secrecy surrounds the trials, funded by the multinational, Monsanto. But one researcher revealed: 'We have got some very angry parents to deal with. Spoilt mothers wailing: "But I hate red hair!" Suspicious fathers glaring at their partners and demanding: "Where did those brown eyes come from?"' The results have also given rise to suspicions of sabotage by anti-genetic engineering activists working as lab technicians or even researchers.

Dr Jones dismisses such suggestions as 'extremely unlikely. I think it more probable that genes are less manipulable and more prone to mutation than we had imagined. After all, life forms survive thanks to their diversity and capacity to change. Maybe genes are more rebellious than obedient and simply won't co-operate with banal human desires for homogeneity.'

Tehran, Iran

The magazine photo is faded. It dates back to the 1990s, nearly forty years ago. Kobra takes a closer look. Yes, it's definitely her. Although the figure is almost entirely covered in loose black clothing she recognises her own forearm.

She flinches as her eye focuses on the bazooka resting on her shoulder. The sensation of its weight comes back to her as a powerful physical memory.

She was young then, an officer with the National Liberation Army. Seventy per cent of the officers were women, as were 30 per cent of the rank and file. An unusual army, especially for those days. They were the armed section of the opposition, dedicated to overthrowing the Islamic State of Iran, a state particularly oppressive to women.

Strange days. How life has changed. She looks out of her window, over the pile of texts. *Islamic Feminism, Female Perspectives on the Q'oran.* Books with her name on them. Next to them the latest batch of invitations to talk at this or that meeting. Should she carry on or should she retire, let others do the work now? Times have changed. There are plenty of younger women around who can now do it.

She looks at the photo once more, then puts it back in the filing cabinet. For posterity.

Tari, Papua New Guinea

Maera scans the newspaper article, clicks into her e-mail, and starts typing:

What planet exactly is the writer of your last editorial inhabiting?

To suggest that we no longer need 'that anachronistic law against wife-bashing, introduced in the last century, because so few prosecutions have been brought in recent years', is as naive as it is complacent.

How does the writer think we got to the current situation in the first place? Perhaps a short history lesson is in order. In 1987 a PNG Government minister went on record saying: 'We pay for our wives, so we own them and can belt them any time we like.' He was not alone. At around that time 65 per cent of PNG wives were beaten by their husbands. Wife-beating accounted for 97 per cent of domestic violence injuries requiring medical treatment. Things have improved considerably since then, partly as a result of the work of women campaigners. PNG was probably the first country in the world to pass legislation and launch a national campaign specifically to stamp out domestic violence.

Would the writer of your editorial think of decriminalising homicide in her or his neighbourhood if there had been no murders in recent years?

The rights of women are not won once. They have to be won again and again. Women's liberation is a tidal affair. A wave comes and we make progress. Then the tide recedes, we lose momentum and inevitably some of our gains. We have to remain vigilant, always.

Yours
Maera Chan

Gambela, Ethiopia

'Mariam, a man from Cargill is waiting to see you...'

'I've got to get this article for *Green Africa Permaculture News* finished first.'

'He's very persistent,' she pauses, '...and hot, and tired, and skinny. Perhaps I should feed him...'

After a while the man from Cargill is shown into the adobe hut where Mariam works. A solar-powered fan cools the room. He starts sweating profusely.

'You find our climate a bit much?' says Mariam.'

'Yes,' he sighs, wiping his face with his handkerchief. 'It wasn't so bad when everything was air-conditioned...'

'Ah yes, the bad old days. What can I do for you?'

He starts his patter. She's heard it all before. Inputs, fertilisers, genetically engineered seeds, high-yield strains, kill-everything pesticides. Even the odd 'eco-friendly' and 'green' epithet thrown in for good measure.

She lets him run out of steam then says: 'No thank you.'

'But...'

She stands up and walks to the window. 'Look out here a minute. What do you see? Fields full of crops. All sorts of different kinds of food crops which we grow using natural fertilisers and biological pest control. We don't try to get more yields per year than nature intended, and the soil repays us by remaining fertile.'

He gets excited: 'Exactly. But you could be growing so much more and exporting...'

She smiles: 'I think we have been here before, and it didn't work for us then. Why should it now? We women are by tradition Africa's farmers. When monoculture, cashcropping and other so-called "modern" farming methods came to our communities during the last century, the men took over decision-making, with disastrous consequences. But when women started the Green Africa Permaculture Campaign in the first decades of this century it was to try and win back our independence, our self-sufficiency. It was, if you like, our agricultural fight for independence.'

'Yes, and you have been very successful. But you could be even more successful, exporting ...'

'You're having problems with food supply in the North ...' she says.

The man from Cargill shifts uncomfortably.

Mariam continues: 'But maybe that means you have to go back to growing your own food, and go for a more sustainable diet. By the way, did you enjoy your meal?'

'Yes, thank you. But...'

'I'm sorry, I have to get on.'

As he is leaving a friendly, podgy child shouts: 'Goodbye mister!'

He tosses a grumpy 'bye' back.

NEWS IN BRIEF

Rio de Janeiro, Brazil

Social scientists in Rio have concluded that the declining sperm count in humans, first noted at the end of the last century, has actually helped avert a demographic explosion in the densely populated countries of the North. In the words of Dr Judith da Silva, leading researcher on the Sperm 2020 Project: 'There was always far too much of the stuff around anyway.'

Beijing, China

The fifth international conference on religious freedom is being held at Beijing this year. Guest speaker will be the new Dalai Lama, the first time the spiritual leader has been incarnated as a woman. Thousands of Tibetans who are celebrating their independence after more than 70 years of Chinese rule are expected to attend the meeting.

Geneva, Switzerland
The World Health Organisation is celebrating a double 10th anniversary this month. The first marks a decade since the rate of HIV infection started to decline. The second anniversary marks the end of female genital mutilation. 'To our knowledge this practice is now extinct,' said a WHO spokesperson.

El Paso, Mexico
Women workers have taken over two more of the city's garment factories this week.

Management have been forced to agree to a co-operative structure partly in response to consumer pressure. One international buyer explained: 'Today's consumer does not simply want to buy a shirt. She wants to know that the shirt she buys has been made under conditions that are fair, democratic and just.'

Dublin, Ireland
The Irish Head of State has announced that she will be accompanied by her same sex partner and their daughter on her forthcoming tour of South East Asia.

She can expect a warm reception in Thailand, a regional leader in the campaign for sexual equality. But in Malaysia the atmosphere is likely to be more tense. Up until the turn of the century the 'crime of homosexuality' incurred a prison sentence of 20 years. Today attitudes have softened but Malaysia still refuses to sign an international accord making discrimination on the grounds of sexual orientation illegal.

Bombay, India
There are plans to change laws on gender prediction of foetuses, following a sharp decline in the male birth rate.

'More and more people want girls,' said a spokesperson from a leading Bombay clinic. 'They are generally seen as more gratifying and less trouble. The superior performance of girls in education also makes them more likely to be able to provide for their parents in old age.'

It's a very different picture from the 1990s when the same Bombay clinic reported that of the 8000 abortions carried out only one involved a male foetus.

Vatican City, Italy

The Pope has overruled centuries of Catholic tradition by endorsing a woman's right to contraception by whatever method she chooses. This appears to be in response to a campaign led by a group of Latin American women priests who have drawn attention to the continuing high rate of maternal mortality in the countries of the South due to lack of family planning. But according to some Vatican watchers the announcement has been timed to deflect attention from the case of Monsignora Maria Paglia, anti-celibacy campaigner who recently admitted to having had 'loving sexual relationships with members of both sexes'. In a recent interview she described her activities as 'perfectly normal' and a 'celebration of the wonderful complexity of God's creation'.

FROM *QUINTESSENCE... REALIZING THE ARCHAIC FUTURE:* A RADICAL ELEMENTAL FEMINIST MANIFESTO

Mary Daly

In *Quintessence...Realizing the Archaic Future,* first published in 1998, Mary Daly exposes and examines the abuses women face at the end of the twentieth century, and she also offers a 'Far-Out Vision of Hope for Wonderlusting Women' who are beginning to discover Quintessence: Spirit that fills the universe and gives it life and vitality.

Her book has been a profound influence on the Anonyma Network, a group of Wild Women who have steadily refused to close their eyes to reality. During the years after the turn of the millennium, they continued their activism – especially their psychic activism – and kept their Eyes and Ears open. As their Foreknowing of the coming Earth Changes became more and more focused and clear, they prepared to leave their homes. At exactly the right Moment, about five thousand of these Foresighted women of all ages and ethnic origins from every part of the Earth began a Journey. Many brought their young Daughters and their Familiars. The women followed their inspired Sense of Direction. They had packed their essential belongings, including their most treasured books, as well as tools and building supplies. Early in 2018, by a series of multiple 'coincidences', they arrived on a small, beautiful continent. They built simple homes, growing their own food in the lush and verdant place. They had Discovered a New and Ancient world that may have been Atlantis. They called it Lost and Found Continent.

It is Now 2048 BE[1] – after great environmental disasters and drastic Earth Changes. Big Brother and his necrotechnology have been soundly defeated. The Anonyma Network, represented by a young philosopher known affectionately as Annie, publishes a Fiftieth Anniversary Edition of *Quintessence*. In order to better understand Mary's complex but extremely joyful and affirming view of women, Annie conjures the author's spirit to engage in a series of conversations about women in the 1990s, and to introduce her to the marvels of the twenty-first century. These discoveries form the basis of Annie's Cosmic Comments, reproduced after each of Mary Daly's chapters, in the 2048 BE edition of the book.

Cosmic Comments and Conversations in 2048 BE Concerning Chapter Five

by Anonyma

A group of my Anonyma Network friends were sitting on the beach engaged in intense discussion about the fifth chapter of Mary Daly's book, Quintessence... Realizing the Archaic Future. *Many of us were in a state of nearly uncontrollable rage, especially as we talked about the genetic manipulation of species that preceded the Earth Changes and our great migration to Lost and Found Continent.*

'And to think how they claimed that animals don't suffer!' roared Anowa. 'The stupidity and arrogance of those men!'

'And of the women who went along with it!' groaned

Sung Hee. 'It's hard to understand how the animals could ever forgive the "human species" for its torture and destruction of the Earth's creatures.'

'It was especially hideous that they "created" monstrously deformed creatures – invading their genetic core,' said Myoko.

Some of us were openly sobbing, not just for women but in some sense even more for the animals, who were not at all complicit in the horrible crimes against nature. I looked around at our Familiars who were clustered nearby, staring at us intently. Just a few minutes before our discussion they had all been going about their own business. Some had been playing happily. The seals had been barking and splashing; the parrots had been swooping among the trees; the snakes had been amusing themselves by hissing at invisible enemies; the rabbits had been hopping among the bushes.

This scene of peace and joy was transformed now into a solemn and silent ritual of listening and watching. The eyes of some of the animals were especially disconcerting, most tellingly the eyes of the pigs and the monkeys. It wasn't that they were angry. That would have been endurable. But instead they expressed an unfathomable sorrow. And beyond that they communicated...sympathy.

'They seem to be telling us that they forgive us,' said Nassrin.

The scene was almost unbearable. None of us younger members of Anonyma had even been 'there' before the Earth Changes, since we had either been born here on Found Continent or had come over as children. The older members, like Kate who had been a student in the late twentieth century, had been deeply repelled by the atrocities and had tried to expose and resist them.

Instinctively I turned to Kate. 'How are you feeling?' I asked softly.

'Terrible,' she replied.

'But you fought and worked to oppose the evil,' I began.

'Not hard enough' was all she could say. We knew that nothing would have been enough, so we waited for her to continue.

Kate looked around at the expectant group. After a while she smiled. The mood in the group subtly shifted. 'Maybe we can do more Now,' she said. 'We are, after all, in the Fifth Dimension, which means that – upon occasion – we can communicate rapidly in Time and Space. And Annie has moved us further along by Invoking Mary, who can bring our messages back to her contemporaries. Then they can have an idea of how their times and their actions look from our perspective.'

'So they can be influenced by us, if they choose to be,' said Sophie. 'Kate, are you saying that we can change the past?'

There was a surge of interest and energy emanating from the crowd of women. I glanced around at the animals and noticed that they were becoming excited. Some of the monkeys and parrots began chattering, and a few cats were frolicking in the tall beach grass. A kookaburra laughed. Nevertheless, they were all listening carefully to every word.

'We can't force anyone or anything,' said Kate. 'But we can attract attention to certain ideas and possibilities, and to the vast Transtemporal context. We can communicate our experiences, and we can beckon and warn.'

'And you can give hope and energy and inspire us to bonding and action in Sisterhood,' commented Mary Daly, who came ambling into the group as an uninvited guest.

Everyone made some welcoming remarks, all at once. 'Well, hello!' I shouted. 'I was just thinking of Invoking you.'

'"Just thinking" is sometimes enough,' responded our guest. 'I couldn't wait any longer for you to get around to issuing me a formal invitation.' She then took a place on the sand next to Kate. 'Please continue, Kate,' she said.

'No, you continue,' Kate laughed. 'I like the part about inspiring you to bonding and action in Sisterhood.'

'Well, yes. I think that is the core of what you are doing,' said Mary. 'Every time I return to 1998 after these visits my friends bombard me with questions. You know how it was at that time, Kate. You were there, then. So many women seemed to have amnesia about patriarchy, even though – or rather, especially because – we were drowning in it. "Sisterhood" often seemed to have been demolished, and there was widespread exhaustion and discouragement. When I tell them about you they say: "So there is hope! There is a Future Sisterhood. We were right all along. We won't be defeated after all!" And that reawakens Vision and Courage.'

Kate was silent for a few minutes. Then she spoke calmly. 'When I think of how it felt to be living then, I remember the sensation of being absolutely overwhelmed. For example, as word came out about the sickening effects of genetically engineered foods, some women were afraid to eat anything or to give their children food from a local supermarket. Almost everything was suspect as unsafe to eat or drink. And there was an unnatural proliferation of strange viruses and bacteria. Even when we decided not to "fixate" on this, it was contributing to our overall anxiety. We all knew that it was important to act. *But there were so many escalating crises toward the end of the century that it seemed there were hundreds of buttons we needed to push, all at the same time! We each had to figure out what our own priorities were...and Name the connections.'*

'What did you think was the most urgent crisis?' asked Anowa.

'On the deepest level, genetic manipulation was probably the worst assault against nature, and perhaps it was the most far-reaching in its destructive implications,' replied Kate. 'But this can't be understood if it is seen as disconnected from the widespread resurgence of

fundamentalist misogynism and terrorism against women. And there was the horror of sweatshop conditions around the world imposed by the United States government, the Third World governments, the Big Business elites, the International Monetary Fund, NAFTA, *and so on. And* that *was connected with the worldwide escalation of female sexual slavery, since many poor women were forced to sell their bodies. At the core of all this was a fanatic phallic lust to own, control, and manipulate life. The fact is that all of the atrocities against women and nature were deeply interconnected.'*

Anowa pursued: 'So how did you decide where to put your energies?'

'The important deciding factor was often personal inclination,' Kate replied. 'My point about the profound interconnectedness of the atrocities was to stress the importance of every well-focused Biophilic action, no matter how small it may have seemed. Each such act strengthened our capacity to Realise the flow of the Archaic Future into our minds at that time.'

'And this enlarged our consciousness,' added Mary. 'To take one huge example, it enabled some of us to continue seeing through the nectech empire's self-justifying propaganda. This became increasingly difficult as the governments, allied with Big Business and Big Science, poured out more and more Lies.'

'I'm interested in pursuing the subject of the connection between such giant Lies and the demonic dissociation you have written about, Mary,' said Kate. 'My own experience was that many of the women I knew back then seemed to become divided by such a maze of deception. For example, in the late nineties fewer and fewer women seemed to be able or willing to Name patriarchy *as the fundamental and all-encompassing system of oppression. Some fixed their attention on "Western civilisation" as the main culprit. There was, of course, good reason to focus on Western civilisation, but the concomitant nonnaming of*

patriarchy narrowed vision, so that connections couldn't be seen.'

'For example,' said Mary, 'it became difficult for many to Name the connections between the escalating oppression of women by fundamentalist movements and regimes around the world and the violation and destruction of women and nature by the nectech empire. The subsequent failure to connect deep ecological concerns with Radical Feminist insight was debilitating.'

'And that's why you issued your book as A Radical Elemental Feminist Manifesto*!' said Sung Hee.*

'Sure,' Mary replied. 'The French Feminist Françoise d'Eaubonne coined the term eco-féminisme *(*ecofeminism*) in the early 1970s in her book* Le Féminisme ou la mort *(*Feminism or Death*). But I have always thought that term isn't strong enough. The word* Gyn/Ecology *says what I mean to say. The expression* Radical Elemental Feminism *spells out further the idea that* Radical Feminism *implies* Elemental Feminism. *That is, it is impossible fully to have one identity/commitment without the other.'*

'But you were not split off from the women who called themselves "ecofeminists"?' asked Myoko.

'Definitely not,' said Mary. 'I respected the commitment and analyses of the women who used different terms. But I kept on trying to invent and retain words that I thought could enlarge the scope of vision and Name connections, so that we could continue to make our analysis deeper, and reach the roots of the problems.'

'The inherent integrity of Radical Elemental Feminism became more and more obvious by the turn of the century,' said Kate. 'Feminist scholars had been aware for some time that women were being cut off from our procreative powers by medical "professionals". The witchcraze of the fifteenth, sixteenth, and seventeenth centuries in western Europe, which targeted women

healers and midwives for violent death, was followed in the eighteenth century by the takeover of midwifery by "man-midwives" with their destructive forceps. In the nineteenth century "gynecology" was invented in order to control women's powers, and towards the end of the twentieth century the "new reproductive technologies" further diminished female self-knowledge and self-esteem. Connected with this was the fact that in the 1990s women's reproductive freedom was being taken away. By 1998, the twenty-fifth anniversary of Roe versus Wade, *which had been a triumph for Free Choice, it had become increasingly difficult and dangerous for women to obtain an abortion. And in the 1990s the bioengineers were "creating" seeds and plants with no self-regenerating abilities. Animals, plants, and women were violated and castrated in the deepest sense by the nectech empire. It became ever more evident that the cause of women and the cause of nature were the same.'*

'It is instructive to look back at reactions to the cloning of Dolly the sheep,' added Mary. 'In 1997 the most blatant patriarchs dispassionately stated that cloning of animals was acceptable but that humans should not be cloned. Their hypocrisy was obvious. Almost all the Feminists I knew were deeply repelled by such arrogant indifference to the fate of animals. And we all knew that if "they" had not already cloned humans, they would soon attempt to do so. Our instinctive knowledge of our deep bond with all of nature was undeniable.'

'I'd like to get back to our original discussion of how we, as your Future Foresisters, can help you and your "Cronies" Now,' I said. I guess it would be helpful if we communicate the fact that you are not a cognitive minority, as you may have imagined yourselves to be. After all, we are Here, as are Foresisters of more ancient patriarchal times and from the Archaic Past. Seen in this wide Transtemporal context, you belong to the cognitive majority.'

At this point in our conversation something wonderful began to happen. All of the carefully listening animals came closer and sat or stood among us. The women who were sitting next to each other shifted positions to make space between them for the animals. A beautiful turtle nudged her way between Kate and Mary, who greeted her warmly. A wombat crouched next to Suzanne, who addressed him as 'Sweet Pea.' A wild boar sat squarely between Anowa and Sung Hee, who both squealed in delight. While a small dog named Ricki nuzzled her friend Kay, a parrot whom I had seen flying around from time to time hopped on my shoulder and began gently nibbling my ear. Many others came and swelled our ranks.

We Time-traveling Cronies well understood that the animals were saying they belong to this majority. Or rather, to put it more accurately, they were inviting us to join their *cognitive majority, which includes plants, rocks, planets, stars, angels – all Biophilic beings. They wanted to communicate their message not only to us but to* their *Foresisters. They were saying that our souls' work is* their *souls' work too, and that we have won. Telepathically we heard and joined in their chorus: 'We* have *overcome!'*

Then we all relaxed and listened together to the powerful symphony of the cosmos. The wind blew in cadence with the cosmic concert, swishing through the trees, whose branches moved in harmony with the celestial music. It danced through the grasses and sands and ruffled feathers, fur, and hair: It stirred the waves of the sea, which roared mightily.

As we listened to this concert and watched the dance of synchronicity we gazed at the glorious sunset. Soon the moon, planets, and stars became visible. Everything in the sky seemed to twinkle rhythmically with the whole symphony.

Everyone knew that this concordance is the vibrating light, sound, and breath of Quintessence, and that it is ultimately Unconquerable. And Now we send this joyful message and Memory of the Future to our Sisters of all kinds and all times so they too can always remember it.

Note

1 BE: became widely accepted, after 2018, as a replacement for the obsolete AD and CE. BE (Biophilic Era) signifies the end of the necrophilic era, that is, patriarchy. The Anonyma Network didn't bother to renumber the years, partly because this would involve tedious complexity, but especially because they wished to signify their bonding and continuity with all the Foresisters who lived in the age of Big Brother.

CONTRIBUTORS' NOTES

Yasmin Alibhai-Brown is an ex-Ugandan Asian who came to Britain in 1972. She has been a lecturer in adult education; has trained unemployed migrant women; and is now a journalist, writing for various publications including the *Independent* and the *Guardian*. She is also a broadcaster and author. Her most recent book is an autobiographical account, *No Place Like Home*, and her next publication looks at the position of women as we enter the twenty-first century. She is a research fellow for the think tank at the Institute for Public Policy Research, where she has a book on race and government forthcoming. She has two children: a 20-year-old son and a five-year-old daughter.

Judith Arcana's work has appeared recently in *ZYZZYVA*, *Nimrod: International Journal*, and *CALYX*; poetry and prose are forthcoming in 1999 in *Fireweed: Poetry of Western Oregon*, *13th Moon*, and a Cleis Press anthology of Jewish women's erotica. She is the author of *Our Mothers' Daughters* and *Every Mother's Son*, published by The Women's Press. Her most recent book is *Grace Paley's Life Stories, A Literary Biography*; she is currently working on a series of poems about abortion. A longtime teacher of women's studies, writing and literature, 50 years resident in the Great Lakes region of the USA, she moved to the Pacific Northwest in 1995.

Vanessa Baird was born in Brussels in 1955 of Anglo-Belgian parents. Since 1987 she has been a co-editor with the development magazine, *New Internationalist*, based in Oxford. During this time she has edited issues on a wide range of themes including feminism in the 1990s, the future, the arms trade, gay rights, the body, Tibet and Mozambique. Before that she worked as a reporter on the *Lima Times* in Peru, covering stories such as the war with Shining Path guerrillas and the drugs trade. In her spare time she writes fiction.

Rosalie Bertell, Ph.D., GNSH, is President of the International Institute of Concern for Public Health (IICPH) and Editor in Chief of *International Perspectives in Public Health*. She earned a doctorate in Biometry at the Catholic University of America in 1966, and has since been working in cancer and birth defect research, with specific emphasis on the associated environmental factors. She is the author of the *Handbook for Estimating the Health Effects of Exposure to Ionizing Radiation* (1986); *Chernobyl: The Environmental Health and Human Rights Implications*; and the groundbreaking *No Immediate Danger: Prognosis for a Radioactive Earth* (The Women's Press, 1985); as well as more than a hundred articles, papers and poems. She is a member of the Grey Nuns of the Sacred Heart, and in 1998, she became President of the Association of Contemplative Sisters.

Rosalie Bertell has received five honorary doctorates since launching IICPH in 1984 and numerous awards, including the Alternative Nobel Prize: Right Livelihood Award, the World Federalist Peace Award and the United Nations Environmental Programme, Global 500 Laureate.

Shelley Bovey is Welsh, an important part of her identity. She worked for BBC Radio 4 for several years before leaving in order to have more time to write.

She now enjoys both writing and broadcasting, though she prefers radio to television because she believes that what you say is more important than how you look. She is a contributor to the *Guardian*, the *Independent* and several magazines and the author of three books. Her polemic, *The Forbidden Body: Why Being Fat Is Not a Sin*, is the seminal British work on size politics and has helped hundreds of women to emerge from the closet of shame. She is editor of a forthcoming anthology of essays by large women for The Women's Press. She lives in Somerset, near Glastonbury Tor, and her greatest passion is her family.

Zelda Curtis was born in 1923 of immigrant parents. Politically active from an early age, she was deeply impressed by the initiatives and activities of the new young feminists in the early 1970s, and became involved in older women's projects and represented their views on the GLC Women's Committee and Islington's Women's Committee. Now, as Chair of AGLOW (Association of Greater London Older Women), she is involved in confidence building and communication skills training for older women, and in campaigning against ageism. A journalist in her working life, on newspapers and magazines, she has also contributed to a number of published anthologies.

Mary Daly describes herself as a voyager, moving beyond the imprisoning mental, physical, emotional, spiritual walls of the State of Possession; a Positively Revolting Hag, repelling the forces of patriarchy; and a Crafty Pirate, Righteously Plundering treasures of knowledge that have been stolen and hidden from women and struggling to Smuggle these back in such a way that they can be seen as distinct from their mind-binding trappings.

She holds three doctorates, including doctorates in theology and philosophy from the University of Fribourg, Switzerland. An associate professor of theology at Boston College, she is the author of *Beyond God the Father: Toward a Philosophy of Women's Liberation, Gyn/Ecology: The Metaethics of Radical Feminism, Pure Lust: Elemental Feminist Philosophy, Webster's First New Intergalactic Wickedary of the English Language* (in cahoots with Jane Caputi), *Quintessence... Realizing the Archaic Future: A Radical Elemental Feminist Manifesto, Outercourse: The Be-Dazzling Voyage,* (all published by The Women's Press), and *The Church and the Second Sex.*

Andrea Dworkin is the author of many books of radical feminist theory, including *Intercourse, Pornography: Men Possessing Women, Right-Wing Women* and the recent *Life and Death: Unapologetic Writings on the Continuing War Against Women.* She has also published the novels *Ice and Fire* and *Mercy.* She is the co-author of legislation recognising pornography as a violation of the civil rights of women. She lives in Brooklyn, New York.

June Jordan is a poet and Professor of African American studies at UC Berkeley, where she also directs the Poetry for the People program. Her most recent titles include *Kissing God Good-Bye* (poetry), *Affirmative Acts* (new political essays), and *Portrait of The Poet As A Little Black Girl,* her forthcoming childhood memoir.

Anees Jung spent her childhood and adolescence in Hyderabad, formerly a princely state of India. Her father, a minister in the court, was a renowned scholar and poet, as is her mother. She inherits the literary tradition from them. She left for the United

States when she was awarded the Barbour Scholarship for Oriental Women by the University of Michigan in Ann Arbor, where she received a Masters degree in American Culture. Anees returned to India and started her career as a writer in journalism. She became editor of *Youth Times*, a publication of the *Times of India*, in 1973. She has continued to explore the human condition in her writings for the last 25 years – in her weekly columns in major Indian newspapers and her books, including *When a Place Becomes a Person* (1977), *Flashpoints* (1981), *Unveiling India* (1987), *Seven Sisters* (1994) and *Breaking the Silence* (1997). She was awarded the Harmony Award for best writing in English in 1989.

Kathy Lette first achieved *succès de scandale* as a teenager with the novel *Puberty Blues*. After several years as a singer in a rock band and a newspaper columnist in Sydney and New York (collected in the book *Hit and Ms*) and as a television sitcom writer for Columbia Pictures in Los Angeles, her novels, *Girls' Night Out* (1988), *The Llama Parlour* (1991), *Foetal Attraction* (1993), *Mad Cows* (1996) and *Altar Ego* (1998) became international bestsellers. *Puberty Blues* and *Mad Cows* have both become major films.

Mphoentle Mageza was born in 1974 and spent her formative years growing up in Germany. She is a South African journalist, currently studying towards a Masters degree in Communications at Howard University, Washington DC. She graduated from the University of Cape Town as the first black South African to write a matriculation exam in German as a mother tongue. She is Emma Mashinini's grand-daughter.

Caeia March was born on the Isle of Man in 1946 and grew up in industrial South Yorkshire. She went to

London University in 1964 and graduated in Social Sciences. She has published poetry, short stories and non-fiction articles, but is best known for her novels, all published by The Women's Press – *Three Ply Yarn* (1986), *The Hide and Seek Files* (1988), *Fire! Fire!* (1991), *Reflections* (1995), and *Between the Worlds* (1996). She is also the editor of a collection of women's writing on myalgic encephalomyelitis and chronic fatigue syndrome, *Knowing ME* (1998).

Emma Mashinini was born in 1929. She worked in the textile trade where she became adopted as a trade union official. She then went on to found one of South Africa's biggest black trade unions, the Catering and Commercial Allied Workers Union of South Africa, when she was arrested and detained without charge. She is now president of the Mediation and Conciliation Centre, Johannesburg, and Commissioner for the 1995 Restoration of Land Rights Act. She is the author of *Strikes Have Followed Me All My Life* (The Women's Press, 1989) and co-author of *Women Hold Up Half the Sky* and *A Book of Hope*.

Kate Mosse is a novelist and short story writer and the author of two non-fiction books, *Becoming a Mother* and *The House: A Year in the Life of the Royal Opera House, Covent Garden*, which accompanied the award-winning BBC television series of the same name. Her début novel, *Eskimo Kissing*, was published to widespread critical acclaim in 1996. Her second novel, *Crucifix Lane* – a feminist thriller set in the future – was published in November 1998 and she is currently researching her next novel, which is set in thirteenth-century France. Kate Mosse is also a Co-Founder and the Honorary President of the Orange Prize for Fiction and she is a member of the Arts for Everyone panel of the Arts Council of England. She is the Administrator of Chichester Festival Theatre, the first woman to hold the position. She lives with her partner and two children in West Sussex.

Jenni Murray is a broadcaster and journalist. She is a former presenter of BBC's *Newsnight* and Radio 4's *Today*. For ten years she has been the voice of Radio 4's *Woman's Hour*. She has made numerous TV documentaries both as a reporter and producer. Her book *The Woman's Hour – 50 Years of Women in Britain* was published in 1996. She has written for a number of magazines and newspapers including *Good Housekeeping*, *Options*, the *Guardian*, the *Independent* and the *Observer*. She also writes a weekly column for the *Express*.

Nawal el Sa'adawi is a novelist, psychiatrist and writer. As a result of her literary and scientific writings she has had to face numerous difficulties and even dangers in her life. In 1972 she lost her job in the Egyptian government. The magazine, *Health*, which she had founded and edited for more than three years, was closed down. In 1981 President Sadat put her in prison. She was released one month after his assassination, and her experiences of this time are recounted in *Memoirs from the Women's Prison* (The Women's Press, 1985). From 1988 to 1993 her name figured on death lists issued by certain fanatical terrorist organisations. In 1991, the government closed down the Arab Women's Solidarity Association over which she presided, and stopped the publication of its magazine, *Noon*, of which she was editor-in-chief.

Nawal el Sa'adawi has been awarded several literary prizes, her books have been widely translated, and she is an internationally renowned speaker and lecturer.

Bulbul Sharma is a painter and writer. She has published three collections of short stories – *My Sainted Aunts* (1992), *The Perfect Woman* (1994), and *Anger of the Aubergines* (1997). She has also written and illustrated a book on Indian birds for children. She works as an art teacher for disabled children.

ACKNOWLEDGEMENTS

'Women Worrying in the USA' by Judith Arcana has been previously published, in a slightly different form, in *ZYZZYVA*, Fall 1998.

'Sustainability: The Big Picture' by Rosalie Bertell is adapted from a paper given at the World Order Conference, Toronto, 1997 entitled 'An Optimistic Picture of the United Nations in the 21st Century'.

Quintessence...Realizing the Archaic Future: A Radical Elemental Feminist Manifesto by Mary Daly is published in Great Britain by The Women's Press, 1999, and in the United States of America by Beacon Books, 1998.

'Changing Up the Future of Women' by June Jordan is adapted from a speech given at the University of Minnesota Women's Studies Department, 28 October 1997.